THE COMPLETE PUBL

GYLES BRANDRETH was born in 1948. Since his days as president of the Oxford Union, he has taken part in, and judged, debating contests of every kind. His twelve-and-a-half-hour after-dinner speech is featured in the *Guinness Book of Records* and he has spoken in settings as varied as the House of Lords and working-men's clubs, at international sales conferences and family weddings. He is a well-known broadcaster, familiar to listeners to *Any Questions*, *Just a Minute*, *Call My Bluff*, *Opportunity Knocks* and many other TV and radio programmes. He has sold more than six million copies of his many books. He lives in London.

Overcoming Common Problems Series

Overcoming Common Problems Series

How to Cope with your Nerves
DR TONY LAKE

How to do What You Want to Do
DR PAUL HAUCK

How to Love and be Loved
DR PAUL HAUCK

How to Sleep Better
DR PETER TYRER

How to Stand up for Yourself
DR PAUL HAUCK

Jealousy
Why it happens and how to overcome it
DR PAUL HAUCK

Living with Grief
DR TONY LAKE

Loneliness
DR TONY LAKE

Making Marriage Work
DR PAUL HAUCK

Making the Most of Middle Age
DR BRICE PITT

Meeting People is Fun
How to overcome shyness
DR PHYLLIS SHAW

No More Headaches
LILIAN ROWEN

One Parent Families
A practical guide to coping
DIANA DAVENPORT

Overcoming Tension
DR KENNETH HAMBLY

The Parkinson's Disease Handbook
DR RICHARD GODWIN-AUSTEN

Self-Help for your Arthritis
EDNA PEMBLE

The Sex Atlas
DR ERWIN HAEBERLE

Six Weeks to a Healthy Back
ALEXANDER MELLEBY

Solving your Personal Problems
PETER HONEY

Stress and your Stomach
DR VERNON COLEMAN

Successful Sex
DR F.E. KENYON

Trying to Have a Baby?
Overcoming infertility and child loss
MAGGIE JONES

What Everyone should know about Drugs
KENNETH LEECH

Why be Afraid?
How to overcome your fears
DR PAUL HAUCK

Overcoming Common Problems

THE COMPLETE PUBLIC SPEAKER

Gyles Brandreth

SHELDON PRESS

LONDON

First published in Great Britain in 1983 by
Robert Hale Limited, Clerkenwell House,
Clerkenwell Green, London EC1

First published in paperback in Great Britain in 1984 by
Sheldon Press, SPCK, Marylebone Road, London NW1 4DU

British Library Cataloguing in Publication Data

Brandreth, Gyles
    The complete public speaker.—(Overcoming common
    problems)
    1. Public speaking
    I. Title   II. Series
    808.5′1   PN4121

    ISBN 0–85969–439–9

Printed in Great Britain by
Richard Clay (The Chaucer Press) Ltd,
Bungay, Suffolk

Contents

Contents

Contents

For Paddy and Dabber Davis

Introduction

Learning to speak in public is like learning to cook: anyone can do it – and almost anyone can do it well. Inevitably, not everyone who takes up public speaking is destined to become one of the Escoffiers of oratory, but everyone who is so inclined can acquire the skills and master the techniques required to make a speech that is effective, eloquent and entertaining. Good public speaking, like good cooking, is a craft that can be learnt. It doesn't call for any particular talent, but it does take time and practice and, for beginners, the use of a basic cookbook. That's what I hope I have written.

Accustomed as I am to public speaking, I realize you may never have heard me in action, and since you would clearly expect the author of a book called *The Complete Public Speaker* to know what he's talking about I'd better begin by presenting my credentials.

For half my life I have been speaking in public and getting paid for it. Between leaving school and going to university I spent nine months working in America and, by a series of happy chances, found myself addressing, first, a conference of teachers at the New York Hilton and, next, one thousand girls and fifty nuns at a convent in Baltimore. Since that baptism of fire in the mid-1960s I have given literally thousands of speeches in hundreds of settings in a variety of countries. I even have the dubious distinction of holding the world record for having delivered the longest ever after-dinner speech.

In 1976 I was approached by Action Research for the Crippled

Child, a very valuable and imaginative charity which had come up with the ingenious idea of inviting people to break world records and be sponsored on the charity's behalf in their attempts. The record for the longest after-dinner speech was then held by the Reverend Henry Whitehead who, on 16th January 1874, rose to his feet at the Rainbow Tavern, Fleet Street, and spoke non-stop for three hours.

One hundred and two years later I captured the Reverend Whitehead's title by talking for four hours nineteen minutes. In 1977 I lost my record to the inimitable Nicholas Parsons and in 1978 Action Research persuaded Nicholas and me to do it all over again and speak for as long as we could on the same night at the same hotel but in separate rooms. We each spoke for exactly eleven hours.

He and I shared the record for a few years until I made my final assault on it on the night of 3rd April 1982 at a dinner sponsored by Cockburn's Port in aid of the National Playing Fields Association. I rose to my feet at 9.00 p.m., just as dinner was being cleared away, and sat down again twelve and a half hours later, just as breakfast was being served.

This book will not tell you how to break my world record, partly because I want to hang onto it, but more significantly because in *The Complete Public Speaker* I have tried to offer fairly sound advice and no one in their right mind would counsel an after-dinner speaker to speak for as long as half an hour, let alone twelve and a half!

The ideas and advice you will find in this book spring not only from my own – mostly happy, occasionally terrifying – experiences as a speaker, debater and broadcaster, but also – and quite as importantly – from my experience as a member of the audience. I have had the privilege of listening to and learning from some brilliant speakers – Robert Morley (inspired), Robert Kennedy (inspiring), Iain Paisley (alarming), Mary Whitehouse (disarming), Freddie Truman (unbelievable), Peter Ustinov (unbelievable), Richard Nixon (unbelievable) – and what I've picked up from masters of the craft like these I have done my best to pass on in the pages that follow.

Many of the best speakers I have heard are not well known,

while unfortunately, many of the worst are, and since we tend to learn more from our mistakes than we do from our triumphs, I am sadly unable to acknowledge publicly the majority of the speakers to whom I am most indebted.

This book is intended as a practical guide and, above all else, I hope that you will find it useful. If you have bought or borrowed it in a last-minute panic because you are making your oratorical debut tomorrow night, you may only have time for one chapter – so it had better be the first: it's an A to Z of tips and tricks designed to help you survive the ordeal ahead. (This is a chapter that I would like you to read and *re-read*. Just in case you don't, in Chapter Two I have deliberately repeated – and amplified – the most important lessons to be learnt from Chapter One.) On the other hand, if you've got hold of the book because you're really desperate since you've got to make a major speech in a quarter of an hour from now, you've left it a little late, but let me at least pass on to you the first – and perhaps the best – advice I was ever given on the subject of public speaking: 'Stand up. Speak up. Shut up.'

That just about says it all, but if you've time to spare I hope you'll linger a little longer, turn the page and read on ...

A speech is a solemn responsibility. The man who makes a bad thirty-minute speech to two hundred people wastes only a half hour of his own time. But he wastes one hundred hours of the audience's time – more than four days – which should be a hanging offence.

Jenkin Lloyd Jones

1

THE A-Z OF PUBLIC SPEAKING

Audience Awareness

> The best audience is one that is intelligent, well educated – and
> a little drunk.   Alban Barkley

Alas, as you will discover almost as soon as you take up public
speaking, not every audience is ideal. When the moment comes
for you to get to your feet and address the assembled company
you may not like the look of the audience sitting in front of you,
but remember: it's the only audience you've got and your job –
above all else – is to please it.

Successful public speaking means gratifying the ears, eyes and
minds of the public rather than the ego of the speaker. If at the
end of your speech you hope to see a sea of satisfied customers
beaming up at you, you've got to give them satisfaction. And to
give them satisfaction you've got to know what they want.

Whatever audience you find you have – attentive or restless,
benevolent or bloody-minded, too well educated or too well oiled
– be acutely aware of it. No speech can be completely successful
without total audience awareness on the part of the speaker.

Assess the room in which you are going to speak. Is it so large
and cavernous that you are going to need all your powers of
projection to be heard at all? Is it so small and intimate that your
style needs to be conversational rather than oratorical? Is it so
long and narrow that you have to keep turning from one side to
the other – like an umpire at Wimbledon – to be sure to include

all your audience as you speak? Is it so hot and smoke-filled that you need to remember to have a full glass of water at your side before you start the speech rather than having to ask for one halfway through your public coughing fit? The time to make up your mind as to the approach you sense the room requires is *before* you get up to speak in it.

Assess the audience confronting you. How old are they? (Will your anecdote about meeting the Ink Spots in 1948 mean anything to them?) What sex are they? (Will they appreciate your lurid reminiscences of your National Service experiences in the red-light district of Hong Kong?) How well informed are they? (Is your discussion on the second law of thermodynamics really going to hold their attention?) A sensible public speaker finds out as much as he can about his audience before he prepares his speech. A wise public speaker then *reassesses* his audience when he comes actually face to face with it.

Assess the mood of the occasion. Inevitably different occasions call for different kinds of speech. Addressing a sales conference when the company concerned has just announced record profits is a very different matter from addressing a sales conference when the company has just announced the closure of one of its factories with consequent massive redundancies. Adopting the tone to match the mood of your audience is really a matter of tact on a grand scale. Just as you wouldn't confront a retired couple on their way to a friend's funeral with a raucous and somewhat vulgar joke – unless you happened to be a master of insensitivity! – so too it would be inappropriate to launch your speech with near-the-knuckle knockabout material when clearly your audience needs something much more serious and subdued.

I think it is probably impossible to please everybody all the time, but you should at least try. At the Savoy Hotel a couple of years ago I spoke at a lunch given by a monthly women's magazine and made a light-hearted speech that seemed to please ninety per cent of the audience, but appalled those at the top table. I made the mistake of poking (gentle) fun at the magazine – which was perhaps discourteous since they were our hosts, and was certainly fatal since they had no sense of humour. When I finished my speech, the bulk of the audience applauded enthusiastically, while, on my left, the editor was reduced to tears of rage and, on my right, one of the magazine's contributors rose to her feet and replied to my speech with a blistering/blustering one of her own. The occasion was an unhappy one and the fault was mine: if I had assessed *all* my audience successfully I could have given offence to none and pleasure to most.

Breaking the Rules

You can break all the rules – once you've learnt them.

This is a book about the craft of public speaking. It sets out to explain the fundamental Do's and Don'ts that will help you become a competent and then an accomplished public speaker. The rules you will find in the pages that follow are fairly straight-forward and designed to be of assistance to fairly straightforward speakers of both sexes. (If I write 'he' and 'him' and 'his' it is simply to save the space involved in writing 'he or she' and 'him or her' and 'his or her' each time. Certainly, at least half of the country's best speakers are women. In 1763 Dr Johnson remarked: 'A woman's preaching is like a dog's walking on his hinder legs – it is not done well, but you are surprised to find it done at all.' The same certainly can't be said in 1983.)

As a rule, you would be well advised to stick to the rules – at least at the start of your speaking career. Yes, Ken Dodd can be invited to give a ten-minute after-dinner speech and then keep the audience in stitches for two and a half hours without anyone complaining. And John Cleese can mount the podium at an important sales conference pulling funny faces and doing silly walks, without the managing director throwing a fit. What's more, Frankie Howerd can address a literary luncheon and instead of speaking cogently on his expected theme, stammer hilariously and to no purpose for half an hour. But it's best to leave the exceptions to the rules to the exceptional. Once you have really mastered the craft of public speaking, you will be able to transform it into an art and do as you please. Until then, stay calm, stay sober and read on.

Cutting Your Coat

When preparing your speech, it is clearly vital to consider the material you are going to use with all the care that you can.

Choose material that suits you. Groucho Marx and Winston Churchill – in their very different ways! – were masters of their particular style. Decide what your style might be. Don't attempt great flights of oratorical fluency if you know you're most at home with very few words and simple ones at that. Don't attempt complicated shaggy dog stories if they don't make you laugh and you're liable to forget the punch line anyway. Don't say anything with which you don't feel 'at home' or with which, in your heart of hearts, you don't agree.

Choose material that suits your audience. That doesn't mean just telling cricketing stories at cricket club dinners – that particular audience has probably heard every single cricketing story there is anyway – but it does mean finding material with which your audience will be in sympathy. You want them to *like* you and they won't like you if they don't like what you say.

Never forget the *reason* for your being asked to give a speech. If you're supposed to be proposing a toast, don't get so embroiled in being witty and stimulating that you forget the toast itself. Behind every speech there is supposed to be a purpose – to say thank you, to say 'cheers', to say good-bye, to mark an anniversary, to offer congratulations, to sell a product – and the speech, however superficially dazzling, will have failed if, in the course of it, its fundamental purpose has been obscured.

Don't Drink and Speak

A personal rule of mine is not to touch alcohol before making a speech. There are some professional speakers, on the other hand, who *cannot* speak without a drink (!) and any number of speakers who feel that 'a couple of stiff ones' will help them to relax and give of their best.

Perhaps a glass or two of wine before an after-dinner speech doesn't do much harm, but in my experience drinking before speaking on any occasion is fraught with danger. Alcohol takes away the 'edge' that I believe keeps a speaker on his toes. It dulls his ability to concentrate on the audience and keep in tune with them as he speaks. Worst of all, it makes the speaker think he is vastly more entertaining and interesting than actually he is!

If drinking and speaking is to be disapproved of, then the use of drugs of any kind is certainly out of bounds. If you have to take anything – even Valium – to help you to your feet, you shouldn't be on them. Public speaking can be nerve-wracking, but if you can't manage it without pharmaceutical assistance then it might be wiser not to bother.

Electronic Help

If there's a microphone on hand, then use it – or at least *appear* to use it. People *think* they can hear better if they *see* a speaker standing in front of a microphone.

Wherever you are going to speak, enquire beforehand if a microphone is to be provided and if it is then test it in advance. It won't enhance the start of your speech if you have to open with the words 'Testing ... Testing ... One, two, three, four ...'

In my experience, every microphone is a law unto itself. Some you need to stand close to. Some you need to have at chest height. Some are multi-directional and allow you a little freedom of movement. Others need to be constantly three inches from your mouth if you are to be heard at all. If possible, get to know the microphone you will be using well before you have to use it. Unless you are a would-be night-club comic, don't hold it. Make sure it has a stand and one that is both adjusted to your height and doesn't wobble. If you are provided with a neck microphone – one that is either clipped to your clothes or hangs around your neck – do your best to avoid banging it as you speak.

Some microphones have on/off switches. Make sure yours is on before you launch into your speech, but don't have it on too soon. I was about to speak at a dinner in the North of England once when my host told me confidentially that, in his opinion, most of the audience were bores and all of them were fools. Unfortunately they heard every damning word he had to say about them: the microphone had been switched on as the coffee was served and the hapless host hadn't realized.

If your microphone squeaks, squeals and screams at you, make one joke about it and carry on. If the electronic noise persists, switch off the microphone and make do without. Recently I spoke to the Southend Law Society and hardly had I begun my address when the amplifiers began broadcasting not only my speech, but also messages being transmitted by the local police. The first time this happened, the audience roared its enthusiastic approval, but after a short while the interference became an irritating distraction. Temperamental microphones and talkative public address systems are good for one lone laugh, but the novelty rapidly wears off.

Food for Thought

People want to be entertained by a speaker, but that doesn't mean that he's got to have them rolling in the aisles from start to finish. Whatever you do, give your audience a good time, but try as well to give them something more. All too many speeches are a mixture of old jokes and even older platitudes. If your speeches are free from clichés, congratulations. If your speeches are both fresh and funny, bravo! If your speeches always contain something the audience can take away with them, you've made it! Yours is the speech they will remember.

What 'food for thought' you choose to offer depends, of course, on the type of audience you are addressing and the reason you have been invited to speak to them. However, whatever the context of your speech, a moment of seriousness – which does not mean solemnity – in which you can put over a sincerely held belief or a well-thought-out idea, or some relevant, new and perhaps even exclusive information, will add an element of depth to your speech that will almost certainly enhance it.

Good Looks

No, I am not going to suggest that all successful public speakers need nose-jobs and face-lifts. Physical beauty is not a prerequisite as far as public speaking is concerned. (Lord Goodman, a tremendously effective public speaker, once acknowledged that he looked like 'an amiable gorilla'.) As a public speaker you don't need good looks, but you do need to look good.

When you are performing in public you are putting yourself on show and you owe it to your audience, as much as to yourself, to look your best. Whether we like it or not, people judge by appearances, so that how you look when you get up to speak will affect the way your audience receives you. As a rule, dress as would be expected of you. Since you are going to be the centre of attention, you can make yourself look a little bit special – I sometimes wear a white dinner-jacket, partly because it stands out in the crowd and partly because it was generously given to me by Aquascutum of Regent Street! – but avoid the obviously eccentric. When you've finished you want people talking about what you said, not what you looked like.

How Long?

'How long, O Lord, how long?'

I once heard this plaintive cry muttered by an unhappy guest who could take no more of the speaker's apparently interminable address. The speaker heard the unkind aside and brought his speech to a hurried and very welcome close. This is the sort of position in which no readers of this book should ever find themselves.

Five minutes for a toast, ten minutes for an after-dinner speech and forty minutes for a lecture are the sorts of durations I recommend in round figures. Later I will give more specific advice, but for the moment remember that no one is likely to complain if you speak for less time than was expected, whereas the converse is not necessarily so. However many minutes you may have spoken for, when members of your audience start looking at their watches, you've gone on too long. And when they start tapping them in disbelief, whatever you do, sit down.

Inspiration

As somebody once said – I expect it was Mark Twain: it usually is – 'Genius is ten per cent inspiration and ninety per cent perspiration.'

Your speech will be a success because of the effort you have put into preparing it and the skill you are putting in to delivering it. At the same time, however well prepared you are, you must leave yourself some room for manoeuvre. Among several reasons for only speaking from notes and never reading a speech word for word, is that the read speech will sound wooden because it is wooden. An element of flexibility is important because it will make your speech come to life *here and now*. When a tray of dishes crashes in the kitchen halfway through your speech, you must respond, however briefly, to what has happened. If you carry on doggedly with what you were saying, it will be unnatural and will make your audience feel uncomfortable.

Giving a speech is not like acting in a play where you have an author's lines to speak and you deliver them in the same way every night. Speech-making is much more like cabaret: you know what you are going to say, but the way you say it – and whether or not you add or subtract anything from what you planned to say or modify the way in which you planned to say it – depends on what happens while you are saying it.

All your speeches will call for preparatory perspiration. Not all of them, especially in the early days, will be acclaimed as works of genius, but, even as a novice speaker, always leave room for inspiration.

Jokes
In other books about public speaking you tend to find a section of 'Jokes – Public Speakers, for the use of'. Not in this one. The reason, as you will discover as you read on, is that I have found that for a public speaker, standard jokes, simply told as jokes, don't really work. If they use jokes at all the best public speakers integrate them so completely into the fabric of what they are saying that they appear more as anecdotes than as 'gags'. Humour is essential in most public speaking, but, unless totally relevant and original, 'funny stories' as such tend to make the individual using them sound like a poor stand-up comedian rather than an entertaining and thought-provoking public speaker. (However, if you are determined to consult books of after-dinner stories, anecdotes and quotations, you will find a bibliography on page 139.)

Know Your Subject
Whatever type of speech you are going to make – an after-dinner

speech, an address at a memorial service, a toast to the bride and groom – make sure you know your subject.

With certain kinds of speech-making – lectures, political speeches, television interviews – your audience may be given an opportunity to ask awkward questions, and with all kinds of speech-making the audience will be able to ask questions in their heads.

Don't speak 'authoritatively' on a subject unless you really are an authority. Since we're all of us authorities on 'life' this shouldn't limit your scope but simply prevent you from inadvertently wading into too deep water.

Lecture Circuits

When you have been speaking in public for a few years, when you have been enjoying it and when your audiences seem to have been enjoying it too, you may be tempted to turn 'professional' and earn yourself some pocket money by doing for profit what you have heretofore been doing for pleasure.

The trouble with speaking for money is that it obliges you to give value for money. When you are speaking out of the kindness of your heart, to oblige an old friend or just to boost your ego, you want to do well, of course, but it is not the end of the world if you arrive late, have a streaming cold and make a speech that falls a little flat. When you are being paid to perform, on the other hand, you have *got* to be good. You have got to be on time too. What's more, you've got to seem to be in the best of spirits and the best of health, however ghastly you feel. And if you're speaking after dinner, you've got to eat that dinner first, however unappetizing it looks, and make interesting and interested small-talk to your neighbour, however vacuous his mind and poisonous his breath.

I am making professional public speaking sound so arduous largely because I do it myself and want to frighten off the competition, but also because, rightly or wrongly, more is expected of the professional than the amateur and you will find that once you have accepted payment for making a speech the responsibility lies fairly heavily on your shoulders.

Professional public speaking falls into two distinct categories:

lectures and after-dinner speaking.

If you are going to give a lecture you need to pick a topic you really can master or have a story to tell that really is unique. Once you have chosen your theme (when I began mine were Pantomime and Prison Reform – not on the same night, of course) or had it thrust upon you (when Sir Francis Chichester went out to speak, his audience would have been sorely disappointed had he not talked about his solo circumnavigation of the globe), you wil' need to create a speech like any other, only longer. You should have several versions of your speech, one lasting thirty minutes, one forty and one fifty, so that you can give whoever books you exactly the length of talk they require. You should also, of course, be ready (and able!) to tackle any questions that may be thrown at you and, what's more, be prepared for an extra, apparently impromptu, 'wind-up' lasting five minutes or so for the occasions when question time is announced but the eagerly anticipated questions aren't forthcoming.

Once you've devised your lecture you'd be well advised to try it out on a number of guinea-pig audiences who are not paying for the privilege of hearing you. When you are sure it works – and if you still feel you want to – you will need to set about getting bookings. The simplest way to do this in the first instance is to produce a small brochure, featuring your photograph, your biography, details of what you talk about and quotes from satisfied customers saying how good you are. Send your brochure to anyone you think might be tempted to book you – Ladies' Luncheon Clubs, Townswomen's Guilds, Women's Institutes, the National Housewives' Register, the Rotarians, Round Tables, churches, schools, colleges – and keep your fingers crossed.

Once you have secured a few bookings – and they will almost certainly be for several months ahead because most organizations like to plan their programme of speakers well in advance – you can even set about getting yourself onto the books of a professional speakers' agency. There are a number of national agencies (whose names and addresses are listed on page 141) and several local ones in various parts of the United

Kingdom. Consult the Yellow Pages to find the names of the agencies nearest to you and write to them, telling them all about yourself and inviting them to come and hear you in action. If you're lucky, they'll come. If you're luckier still, they'll like what they hear and put you on their books. This means that you will feature in their brochure and that when the Norwich Young Farmers – or the Cleethorpes Ladies' Circle – want a talk on Philately – or Hang-Gliding or Chinese Cookery for Beginners, or whatever your subject happens to be – the agency will recommend you and take ten or fifteen per cent of your fee for doing so.

To be successful on the lecture circuit you will need to be either famous or unique, or good *and* different. The first Briton to land on the moon will get a lot of bookings because his achievement will make him both famous and unique. Assuming you're not yet a household name and haven't been around the world on roller-skates you will need to be different as well as good only because there are already plenty of good speakers lecturing on all the obvious topics. To be a sought-after lecturer in today's competitive market-place you need a speciality that has general appeal and yet manages to be definitely out of the ordinary.

With after-dinner speaking your 'subject' is not so important. You will be booked because you are known to be entertaining and arresting. As an after-dinner speaker it is difficult to sell yourself: 'word of mouth' is really the only kind of publicity that will get you the bookings you want and there's nothing you can do to secure that except give of your sparkling best each and every time you speak.

Money, Money, Money!

What will you get paid as a professional after-dinner speaker? Well, it could be anything from £20 to £2,000, depending on whether you are Mrs Kendal of the Accrington Dyslexic Association or Dr Henry Kissinger, former United States' secretary of state. The chances are that, unless you're very good or very famous or very lucky, you'll begin at around £30 per speech (plus expenses) and work your way up the financial scale as you get better known and more sought after.

Celebrities who really are household names can command £1,000 or more per appearance, but often ask less if they enjoy speaking and want to do more. Some ask for vast fees specifically because they dread the prospect of a 'personal appearance' in which they must sing for their supper, while others, whom you might expect to be expensive, come relatively cheap because they love the sound of their own voices or want any excuse to get away from home.

Novelty

'Something old, something new, something borrowed, something blue.' What a bride is supposed to have about her on her wedding day turns out to be what most speakers choose to put into their speeches. I must say I can do without the old and the borrowed and the blue – and you would be well advised to avoid them too, if you can – but when I am in an audience I always respond well to something *new*. As an acid test and a devastating exercise in self-discipline, when you have finished preparing your speech, look through it carefully and make sure it contains at least one element – an idea, a piece of information, a story, a way of presentation – that is genuinely new. If it's *all* been said before, then do you really need to say it again? But if you've got something new to offer – and it doesn't need to be much – then your effort is worth while.

Obfuscation is Taboo

As a rule, when speaking in public don't say 'A slight inclination of the cranium is as adequate as a spasmodic movement of one optic to an equine quadruped utterly devoid of visionary capacity' when you could say 'A nod's as good as a wink to a blind horse.' (This rule doesn't apply, of course, if you are a professional politician and you *want* to obscure your message rather than make it crystal clear!) Every member of your audience should understand every word you have to say.

Practice Makes Less Imperfect

Some actors – Donald Sinden for example – occasionally rehearse in front of a mirror. On the whole, I think speechmakers who practise in front of mirrors tend to become self-conscious and overly aware of personal mannerisms. If you are too self-conscious you won't be natural.

Obviously you may need to be a little larger than life when you speak in public, but avoid the over-theatrical and melodramatic. On radio and television, on the other hand, you'd be well advised to be a little 'smaller than life', while not becoming so subdued as to seem somnolent.

Public speakers are like conjurors: to get their effects right they need to practise, practise, practise. But, unlike conjurors, the best practice for public speakers is that done before an audience. Without any doubt, the more often you speak the better you'll get.

Quick, Quick, Slow

Variety is not only the spice of life it is also the essence of good public speaking. Whatever the length and purpose of your speech, vary the pace and vary the tone.

Come what may, don't rush. Novice speakers and nervous speakers have a tendency to dash desperately through their speeches, no doubt hoping to get the ordeal over with as quickly as possible. This is a mistake. Always begin calmly and in an unhurried way. Make sure your audience has settled down before you start. If chairs are being adjusted or coffee cups cleared away, wait for the scraping and the clinking to stop before you begin. When you do speak, be unhurried but never ponderous. Include some faster moments and some slower ones, bring in light and shade, be amusing and serious. In the course of the best kind of speech you should be able to hear uproarious laughter at one moment and a pin drop the next.

Rude Interruptions

Generally speaking the best way to handle hecklers is to ignore them. If you answer them back, there is a danger that your banter may encourage them. Most seasoned speakers have one or two put-downs up their sleeves that can be produced instantly to deal with any rude interruptions, but if you find your first riposte doesn't have the desired effect don't go on. I shall not quickly forget the night at the Piccadilly Hotel in London when my devastating quips, far from felling the drunken interrupter, emboldened him to stagger to his feet and walk over to the top table. There he stood mouthing drunken abuse literally six inches away from me while I struggled on with my speech. Nothing I could say would deter him and since he was apparently the chairman's oldest friend there was nothing that anyone else could do to deter him either!

Don't worry: this sort of thing doesn't happen very often, but when speaking after dinner, if you have a choice in the matter, choose to speak sooner rather than later. If your audience has drunk too much before you get to your feet, they may be literally 'too tired' to be able to concentrate or too merry to want to. I once spoke at a hospital where one of the young doctors at the top table rose to his feet and threw up just as I was rising to begin my address. On another occasion at a dinner in the City of London, I was obliged to stop speaking almost as soon as I had started, because a group of guests had poured brandy over their table-cloth and set fire to it!

Unless you're fully prepared for your speech to become a double act, ignore obstreperous interrupters. Remember the old maxim: silence is the unbearable repartee.

Speak Because You Want To

Only ever speak because you want to. I don't believe anyone – not even fathers of the bride – should be forced to speak if they really can't bear the idea. If you enjoy speaking, show your enthusiasm and your audience will share it. If you don't enjoy it, the chances are your audience won't enjoy it either.

Truth Will Tell

The late Godfrey Winn was a very popular public speaker. I never warmed to his somewhat saccharine style, but his audiences generally loved him. I couldn't quite understand why this was until after his death, when I was invited to take over his weekly column in the magazine *Woman*. Godfrey Winn was a tremendous success as a *Woman* columnist. I was not. The reason, I eventually realized, was that he *meant* what he wrote, whereas I was trying to adopt a style that didn't come naturally to me and with which I wasn't really in sympathy. The same was true of his speaking: it was all too sugary and sentimental for my liking, but it worked for him because he meant it.

Sincerity is vital in a public speaker. Put on an act and they'll see right through you. Say what you believe and feel and know to be true and your audience will listen to you, like you and respect you.

Unique Experience

A unique experience – that's what you want your audience to feel they've had when they have heard you speak. It may be the tenth Golfing Dinner you've addressed this year, but you've got to make your audience feel that it is the first and only one. You will manage to do this if, as well as being fresh and original and acutely aware of your audience, you also throw in one or two relevant and well-observed local references. Your listeners will then feel this speech has been designed specially for them. Add one or two topical references and they will know that you are speaking to them here, tonight, now – not just dusting off the tired old notes you always use for golfing dinners.

Vulnerability

Every public speaker is nervous underneath, and to show a little of your nervousness won't harm you. It may even work in your favour. If you are too self-assured, too confident, too much in command, you may appear arrogant. A modicum of vulnerability can be an asset.

Waterworks

Before you speak, do go to the loo. This will enable you to smarten yourself up, take a last minute look at your notes and speak with your mind on the matter in hand and not on your nagging bladder. Needing to go to the lavatory just before you speak is largely a matter of nerves, but if you feel a call of nature prior to speaking, don't ignore it – or the consequences may be unfortunate. Many years ago when I was president of the Oxford Union, I had to halt the proceedings and ask that marvellous speaker Fanny Cradock, to pause mid-speech while I rushed from the chamber to relieve myself! The sound of the mocking laughter of that thousand-strong audience still echoes in my ears.

Censorship

Whether or not you believe in censorship in general (and what a good subject for a debate it is), self-censorship in the particular case of public speaking is essential. As a rule avoid anything that any *reasonable* member of your audience would regard as offensive. (I stress the word 'reasonable' because of a recent experience of mine. I gave a speech at the Stock Exchange and a couple walked out in a huff when I said that I wouldn't keep the audience long because I didn't want to hold up the serious business of the hour: drinking. Now you can't always be sure your audience won't contain over-sensitive teetotallers, but if you bear the *reasonable* people in mind, you won't go far wrong!)

It goes without saying too – though I shall say it again later in the book – that you should never use bad language in a speech or make remarks that could be construed as racist or slanderous.

Your Very Good Health

However brilliant you are, however experienced, however much time and trouble – and talent – you have put into preparing your speech, just once in a while you'll be faced with a disaster. When things really have gone wrong and you realize there's no way you can save the day, don't despair. Propose a toast instead. It will be a surprise toast and you will only be able to propose it if you have already found out the name of the most loved and respected individual in the room. By asking your audience to get to their feet and join you in drinking to the health of good old so-and-so, you divert attention from yourself and on to someone towards whom your audience is always eager to show affection. The audience will like you for liking one of their number and respect you for showing your respect to their most respected member! What's more, in order to join you in the toast, your audience will have to get to their feet, and if they start applauding while still standing you'll find that speech you feared was a flop, a frost and a fiasco, is culminating in a standing ovation!

Zest

The quality I believe the public speaker needs almost above all others is *energy*. If you've never spoken in public before, when you do you will be amazed by what an exhausting experience it can be. When you sit down after even a fairly brief speech you may well find yourself completely drained.

Public speaking calls for considerable reserves of energy – physical, mental and nervous. The night before you are due to give an important speech, you'd be better advised to get to bed early than burn the midnight oil polishing your speech which, if it isn't ready then, never will be. To give an effective speech you need to feel fresh, you need to be on the ball, you need to be ready for anything. My motto is: to be at your best, you need zest. Good luck!

2

LEARNING THE CRAFT

Public speaking is a craft and like any craft it has to be learnt, practised and developed. Ralph Waldo Emerson was of the opinion that 'All good speakers were bad speakers at first,' and it is certainly a fallacy that public speakers are born and not made.

Obviously some people are more adept than others, but, by following simple guidelines, *anyone* can become an accomplished public speaker. Sir Winston Churchill, often described as the greatest orator of our time, once admitted that he found making speeches 'very, very hard work' – and if a speaker of his stature had anxieties, no-one will condemn you for yours.

Whether you are making an after-dinner speech at the Savoy, addressing the annual general meeting of the Poole Branch of the Anti-Vivisectionist League, or simply saying a few words to the guests at your third 21st birthday party, there are ten basic rules you should bear in mind before you start.

The Rules of Public Speaking

1. Be human. You know that you are human, but don't keep it a secret. Your audience can see that physically you have the usual number of arms and legs, but you must show them that you have a heart as well, that underneath the dinner-jacket, or stunning evening gown, there is a friendly heart beating and that the personality therein is not merely warm as a result of thermal underwear.

Imagine yourself in the position of your audience. To whom would you rather listen – one who appears overly grand, condescending and in a class of his own, or someone who seems a natural and approachable person, whom you would like to know better?

Speakers frequently fall into the trap of trying to place themselves *above* their audience. Of course, it is an honour to have been asked to speak, but you do not suddenly become royalty because of it. The simplest way to create the right atmosphere is to *be yourself*. Don't be pretentious and do try to appear relaxed; your listeners will accept you much more readily and respect you for it.

The opening of your speech is, of course, vital – and will be dealt with in detail later – but it is worth remembering here that with your first few words you can show your audience how human you are. You must never seem remote or superior. It is impossible to go wrong with a light-hearted opening designed to endear you to your audience: 'Whenever I listen to other people's speeches, a funny thing always seems to happen to the speaker on the way to an engagement. Funny things never seem to happen to me like that ... until tonight! I'd just got into my car ...'

Take your audience into your confidence. Be personal, be revealing, be human.

2. *Keep it simple*. In 1715 Alexander Pope wrote that 'simplicity is the mean between ostentation and rusticity'. In other words, if you keep your speech simple you will not appear over-ambitious nor unpolished. Simplicity is the key to a good speech because it enables you to communicate with every listener, and often the funniest things in life really are the simple things – like pickles and snoring. The simpler your subject (if you have a choice) the more easily your listener can identify with it. Everyday events are common to all. Simplicity means not only dealing with an uncomplicated subject but using plain and comprehensible language. Effortless eloquence is one thing, but never use words that you yourself do not understand, or of whose meaning and pronunciation you are unsure of.

3. *Make your speech enjoyable*. A speech, whatever the subject,

is meant to be enjoyed rather than endured. Even the most serious of topics can be coloured to keep the attention of your audience. If humour is appropriate then use it; if a joke or quip would seem in poor taste the speech can still be lightened with personal anecdotes. Everyone likes a story, even if it is serious in content and message, and this can often be the most effective way of underlining an important point.

I heard this at a school prize-giving recently:

'A young boy in his first term at grammar school was devoted to the game of football. His lifelong dream was to be a professional footballer, and one Saturday afternoon he worked his heart out practising his skills. His team coach shouted at him: "Go and sit in the changing-room! You're the worst footballer I've ever seen on this field, now get off."

'At the end of the afternoon the players returned to the changing-room to find the boy crying his eyes out. He hadn't even bothered to take his boots off.

'The coach went up to him, ruffled his hair and said: "Look, son. I meant it when I said that you were a lousy footballer, but I'll tell you something else – and I mean it. One day you're going to be the greatest footballer this country has ever known, and the reason is that you are willing to work, you're prepared to practise, and I know you've got the determination that will enable you to succeed in the end."

'The boy immediately cheered up, he had new heart, and he went out onto the field and practised till the light failed.'

A simple, sentimental and really rather banal story like that can add power to a speech and make it more enjoyable. The speaker could just as easily have said 'Don't let things get you down – don't give up however hopeless the cause may appear – determination will help you succeed in the end,' but the message was made that bit more telling and entertaining.

Most speeches benefit from an injection of humour, and if an audience laughs (with you, not at you!) it is a sure sign that your listeners are enjoying themselves. Why is humour so important?

a) It tells your listeners that you are a friendly and approachable person.

b) It promises enjoyment, so your audience concentrates more.

c) It unites audience and speaker. Humour will get your listeners involved because they *want* to hear what you are going to say next.

d) It will relax the audience, and at the same time will release the tension in you, the speaker. Recently a friend of mine had to make a speech for the first time as a best man at a wedding. He was so tense that he got up to introduce the father of the bride, not noticing that the man had slipped out to the lavatory. As the best man announced him, the father of the bride made a timely and unsuspecting entrance from the door marked GENTS – and the delighted guests all roared. Any tension there may have been evaporated and the atmosphere for all the subsequent speeches was as relaxed as you could hope for.

Study what other people laugh at, and what makes *you* laugh. What are the funniest parts of other people's speeches? Usually the stories of their failures, embarrassments and blunders, the tales of the times they've opened their big mouths and put their foot right in it.

According to Will Rogers, 'Everything is funny if it happens to another person.'

To your audience *you* are the 'other person' and they will enjoy hearing of the calamities that have befallen you over the years. The more personal you are, the more original your speech will be. On the whole, amusing anecdotes based on true-life experience go down far better with an audience than conventional 'gags' culled from joke books, however well told.

4. *Choose material carefully.* Tailor your speech to suit your audience and beware of using anything that is even vaguely offensive. Avoid jokes that are 'sick' or 'blue' and tread warily on the subject of religion. You may think a joke about a Catholic priest and a Rabbi is hilarious, but some of your listeners may be offended or upset. One remark in bad taste could lose you the support of your audience.

As a rule, don't make a joke about something that is so serious that it is risky to laugh about. Jokes about cancer, death and handicaps of all kinds should be avoided. Also be careful not to belittle your audience or make light of things they may take seriously.

5. *Speak loudly and clearly* – and don't rush. It would be something of a tragedy for you to make the greatest speech since Churchill's 'Blood, sweat and tears', and for nobody to hear it because you are inaudible.

Listeners must always be able to hear and understand what you are saying, and this is a matter of both volume and clear diction. Many speeches are ruined because a nervous speaker gabbles or keeps dropping his voice. You don't want to hear members of your audience muttering 'What did he (she) say?' 'I don't know, I couldn't quite catch it ...'

Vary your pace, but never rush your speech. A good speech can be turned into a brilliant one, with polished delivery and the telling use of pauses. When you have a particular message or point to make, use pauses to help you.

Churchillian oratory may not be what you're after when announcing the raffle in the village hall, but it is always possible to learn from a master. This is Winston Churchill in the House of Commons in May 1940:

'You ask [pause] "What is our aim?" [pause] I can answer [small pause] in one word [pause]: Victory! [pause] Victory at all costs, [pause] victory [small pause] however long and hard the road may be, [pause] for without victory [pause] there is no survival.'

Try reading the speech *aloud* both with and without the pauses and you will soon see how much more striking and effective it becomes when properly timed.

The pause should be used in a similar fashion when you are hoping to make your audience laugh – because audiences need time to adjust to a humorous climax.

6. *Plan your speech carefully*. Good organization is essential to a good speech.

Disorder can be your worst enemy, and not only will it make any public speaking difficult for you it will sound unprofessional to your audience. A well-structured speech will flow naturally and should be a joy to listen to.

When preparing a speech this is what you need to do:

i) Choose a theme

What is your speech going to be about? Sometimes you may be asked to give a particular speech on a specific topic, in which case you'd be wise to do broadly as you're asked.

If you're not given a set subject, choosing your own isn't always easy. If you can, make your theme relevant to your listeners and pick a subject that you know something about and will feel comfortable with.

Begin planning your speech as soon as you have been asked to make it. That way ideas will come gradually over a period of time and you will have an opportunity to reject anything unsuitable.

Generally speaking, it is unwise to attempt to formulate your speech on the night before you are due to deliver it. The more time you give yourself the clearer your thoughts will be.

Whatever your theme – Bird Watching in East Anglia, Education in the 1990s, My Life and Other Disasters – write it down in the middle of a piece of paper. Now, literally, write your thoughts and ideas around the central theme.

Jot down odd words, whole sentences, even complete paragraphs. Now look for any suitable quotations. Study the newspapers for topical elements. Try not to wander from the theme, but explore all its possibilities as much as you can.

ii) Build around your theme

Having compiled your list of ideas, perhaps over several days, start to order them. Go through ruthlessly crossing out anything you are unhappy with or that seems too remote from your theme. If you find it difficult to order your thoughts, then divide them into three more lists, treating your subject rather like a journey:

  a) Setting off – all thoughts that lead into your subject.

  b) Arrival – thoughts and ideas that actually deal with your main theme.

  c) Departure – ending your journey and what you have concluded from it.

If you prefer to be more technical you can divide them up into

Introduction, Main Subject and Conclusion.

Having formulated your ideas, put together the stories and personal anecdotes that will help make the speech more entertaining. Inject humour where you can, but only if really relevant and *really* funny.

iii) Pay attention to the opening and closing of the speech
The opening will be your 'attention-grabber'. The ending will give the audience the impression of you that they will take home, so it is important that you exit on the right note.

Many speakers like to write the opening and conclusion to their speech at the same time so that they match up and give the speech a sense of unity. (This is explored more fully in Chapter 3.)

7. *Be sincere*. Ignore anyone who advises you to 'Be sincere – even if you don't mean it!' and talk only from the heart. Sincerity – or the lack of it – can be spotted at once by an audience. If we have it, we will be forgiven many of our shortcomings, if we haven't, we may as well pack up and go home.

8. *Be direct and to the point*. We have all listened to speakers droning on and on monotonously and thought to ourselves: 'For goodness sake, get to the point!'
Don't waffle. Don't be verbose. Don't indulge in time-wasting circumlocution.
If you choose your vocabulary carefully and make direct statements, your impact could be considerable and your chances of boring your audience slight.

9. *Find out who your audience will be*. It is imperative when making any speech to find out who will be in your audience and slant your material, topic, humour and vocabulary accordingly. A story that may be splendid for the Rugby Club Christmas Dinner may not be quite so popular at the Temperance Society Cocoa Evening.

10. *Keep your speech short*. As the saying goes: 'If after ten minutes you don't strike oil, stop boring!' No speech will ever be

criticized for being too short; the same cannot be promised if it is too long! Before you start, and preferably before you prepare your speech, you should find out exactly how long you will be required to speak, and then make every effort to keep inside that limit. Nobody will feel they have had short measure if you finish sooner than anticipated, and the good speaker always leaves his audience wanting more.

When preparing your speech don't forget to make optimistic allowances for audience laughter and applause. If you've got to speak for ten minutes, then prepare eight, and make best use of your allotted time by not repeating yourself and never using 200 words when twenty will do.

Remember the golden rule:

Stand up to be seen.
Speak up to be heard.
Sit down to be appreciated.

Do's and Don'ts of Public Speaking

Do's

1. Do get to the venue at the right time and in the right clothes. If you are late it will make your hosts anxious. If you have to rush you will arrive flustered. If you are supposed to be in a dinner-jacket and you arrive in a lounge-suit you will feel a fool. The more relaxed, comfortable and confident you are, the better your speech will be.

2. Do make sure that you are fully prepared before you make your speech. Are the visual items you need in position? Have you got your contact lenses, or glasses, with you? Do you have your notes handy? Do you know exactly at what point you have to make your speech? Do you know where to stand? Do you know how to control the microphone if there is one?

3. Do you have a glass of cold water within easy reach in case your mouth dries up. Nerves have a habit of making one's throat tighten up, and a glass of water will help. Do not have it in a precarious position so that it might be knocked over either by

yourself or somebody else. But avoid taking too many sips of water, as this is distracting. If, however, you do lose your train of thought a quick – but calm – drink of water may just give you time to find yourself again.

4. Do keep your material and your thoughts to yourself before the speech, without divulging the content to the chairperson or any member of your audience. The last thing you want is for someone to nudge their neighbour because they know a good bit is coming up, or for anyone to go to sleep because they have heard it all before!

5. Do, if you are a first time speaker, try and position yourself where you have sight of a timepiece, or discreetly lay your watch where you can see it easily, so that you can keep within your time limit. The experienced speaker knows beforehand exactly how long his speech will take, but at first it is easy to get carried away and talk too long. Do not, however, keep glancing at your watch.

Don'ts
1. Don't use any jokes that are likely to offend. I know I have said this before, but it is worth repeating. Although people may laugh from a sense of duty, it will probably be embarrassed laughter. At the worst, people will walk out. At a function I attended a speaker told a joke in bad taste about a man in an iron lung. A man and his wife got up and left the room. Their son was in an iron lung ...

2. Don't use a joke or story that you have heard on television. There is a strong probability that the majority of your audience heard it too, and a professional comedian is likely to have told it in his own style and manner, which may not become you.

3. Don't include stories that suggest an intimacy you cannot justify. It can alienate your audience. Avoid saying, 'The other day my wife and I dined with Lord and Lady Knowall ...' when you were one of eight hundred guests at a reception at which Lord and Lady Knowall were present.

Never imply that you know people personally when you do not and – as President Reagan once put it to me – 'avoid name-dropping like the plague'.

4. Don't use complicated stories that listeners might not understand or might misconstrue. Nothing is more unnerving or embarrassing to a speaker than to reach the end of a joke and to find himself confronted by a sea of blank, expressionless faces. It is a situation that should be avoided at all costs, because, wish it though you will, floors do not open up and swallow you out of sight.

5. Don't use a story or joke just because you like it – only use it if it is relevant.

6. Don't ever make yourself the hero of any situation. Give the other fellow the credit: 'So my neighbour suggested that I ... and it worked. Why don't you try it too?'
   That sounds much more human than saying, 'So I thought to myself, the best way to do this is ... and it was a tremendous success.' That will only result in your being credited with a big head, not the best ideas.

7. Don't use dialects in your speech unless you are really competent. The audience will feel embarrassed *for you*. I cringe when I hear a joke about a Scotsman, an Irishman and a Welshman, and the speaker attempts each with an accent that sounds like a cross between a Frenchman and a Pakistani.

8. Don't use phrases that people would not use in everyday speech. I once heard a mayor declare in the course of his speech: 'Who could possibly require such? I proclaimed enquiringly.'
   If he hadn't been a mayor he could have said the same thing so much more effectively: 'Who ever would want a thing like that, I asked.'
   The simpler your language the better.

9. Don't stop if a story falls flat – just carry on with your speech

as if nothing had happened. Never stop in the middle of a speech simply because you feel that it is not being appreciated. Should it for any reason be necessary – the building happens to be on fire; World War III has just been declared – bring it to a premature close using your intended conclusion, but always complete a speech if you can.

10. As a general guide don't speak for more than fifteen minutes at the absolute outside. After-dinner speakers usually feel that around twelve and a half minutes is an ideal length for both speaker and listener.

How to Take Your Position

It may sound the easiest thing in the world to walk on to a platform or mount a podium – but the problem is timing. *When* do you stand up? Before you are announced? As you are announced? Or after you have been announced?

This somewhat depends upon your location. Obviously if you are seated at the back of the hall you are going to need more time to reach your position than if you are sitting at the foot of the platform steps. At a luncheon or dinner you may only have to rise to your feet – and there you are.

Ideally the time to stand up is almost immediately you have been introduced. Count to five, and then rise. This gives just a moment of anticipation, but keeps movement within the room and does not leave the chairman standing too long waiting for you to arrive.

If you are speaking from a podium it is important that it is never left unattended. The person who has introduced you should remain there until you arrive and then step back gracefully. Likewise, when you have finished, do not walk away immediately but wait until the next speaker or the Chairman arrives to take over. This avoids any unnecessary traffic jams with subsequent speakers.

How to Stand

Inexperienced speakers tend to hold themselves stiffly, which looks and feels unnatural.

But resist the temptation to go to the other extreme and slouch. Stand upright, with your weight distributed evenly on both feet. In this way your posture will be more comfortable and your legs less likely to ache. If you must shift your weight from foot to foot, put the pressure on the ball of the foot, rather than the heel, and you will be able to change the weight without drawing attention to the fact.

What to Do With Your Hands

Apart from being used to make the occasional gesture and to hold notes, hands can be a nuisance. In *The Devil's Dictionary* Ambrose Bierce defined a hand as 'a singular instrument worn at the end of a human arm and commonly thrust into somebody's pocket'. Devil's definition indeed, for in public speaking the last place your hands should be is in your pockets.

Most of us take little notice of our hands, until, that is, we have to speak in public, and then they appear uncommonly large and obtrusive. So, what should you do with your hands?

1. If the podium is high (at chest level) then rest your hands lightly on either side. If you are at a table, *don't* rest your hands as this will give you very bad posture and make your delivery difficult.

2. If you have notes hold your hands at around waist level. If you are right-handed, hold your notes in that hand and let your left hand lightly grasp your right wrist. This is a particularly comfortable position to adopt and most speakers can stand in that position throughout their speech.

3. If you have no notes then clasp your hands together, fingers entwined, and let them hang loosely in front of you. Forget the old school of thought that arms should be held loosely by your sides – this looks too false.

4. Some men (for instance the Duke of Edinburgh) can get away with clasping their hands behind their back, but generally this looks uncomfortable.

5. As a rule, don't fold your arms in front of you. This appears casual and sloppy, and can suggest a gossipy appearance, as though you are nattering over the garden fence rather than addressing a room full of people. Looking relaxed and at ease is one thing, but your audience won't be flattered by excessive informality.

If you can use a variety of arm movements during your speech, it will prevent you looking too tense, but don't overdo it, and remember that sudden changes can be distracting.

Mannerisms

The basic rule with mannerisms is *avoid them altogether*. While it might be fun to have a Groucho Marx cigar or a lorgnette 'just to be different', the eyes of your audience will be on your props rather than on you – and that will never do.

Watching a speaker when he or she fiddles with a button, runs his fingers up and down the stem of a wine-glass, or twists a necklace or ring every few minutes, can be very irritating. So make sure you have no annoying habits. If you can face the truth, the simplest way to do this is to ask a close friend to let you know if you have any distracting mannerisms and what they are.

Your Appearance

Before you have even opened your mouth, how you look and dress say a great deal about you as a person – so decide what you want to communicate about yourself.

Obviously you want to dress appropriately for the occasion. If it's a formal wedding or a black-tie dinner you will go dressed accordingly. Always check beforehand, because it won't help your speech at the Guildhall if you are wearing a checked sports jacket and kipper tie if your audience is dolled up to the nines in white tie and tails.

Similarly, avoid anything ostentatious or outrageous. It is your speech – not your outfit – that should bring the audience to its feet.

You want to dress in a way that will enhance the aura of calm authority you are hoping to exude. You may feel like a jelly inside, but you ought to look like the Rock of Gibraltar. If you look good and are dressed comfortably, you will feel good and comfortable. Don't have big bulges in your pockets (this might look as though you've brought your sandwiches with you). If you are using notes, make sure you know just where they are: this will prevent confused fumbling as you search for them.

How to Use Notes

Unless you happen to be a president or a prime minister (in which case you want no advice from me) where every word counts and your script can be discreetly unrolled before your eyes so that you see it but the audience doesn't, *never read your speech*. The spoken word is different from the written word and if you prepare a text and then read it out word for word, you will give the impression of someone reading a newspaper article out loud – and that's not what public speaking is all about.

By the time you rise to make your speech you will be so familiar with what you want to say that you won't need to read it. You may need notes to keep you on the right track, but they should only consist of bald headings.

Many speakers put their notes on postcards. The only danger here is that you may drop the cards just as you are about to speak and gather them up in a frenzy – and in the wrong order. You may also inadvertently discard two cards at a time and suddenly find that you have skipped the heart of your speech. If you can fit all your notes onto one side of one piece of paper that, I think, is the safest course.

One distinguished after-dinner speaker once commented that notes should be used as gems of wisdom rather than as a crutch for your weak memory.

So don't try to hide them, or give the impression that you are craftily looking at them to refresh your memory – use them openly. Don't, for example, bend your head down to look at your notes, instead lift the notes up so that you can read them.

Never step away from the podium to look at your notes. This makes much too big an issue out of it and is unprofessional. Obviously nobody's memory is infallible and if you have a special quote that you would like to use, no one will object if you read it. You can even say something like:

'In 1873 Benjamin Disraeli said at a banquet in Glasgow a few words which I feel are particularly applicable to myself on this occasion. He said (*lift up your notes and read*): "An author who speaks about his own books is almost as bad as a mother who talks about her own children." '

In this way you have made no apology for using notes. You simply look as though you've done your homework.

Obviously try not to rely too heavily on notes: they are just small reminders to keep you on the right course and cannot take the place of good preparation.

The more speeches you make the more your memory will develop and the less you will need notes. And don't worry if at the end of a speech you find you have forgotten to say something you had intended. Remember A.P. Herbert's consoling counsel: 'If you forget what you are going to say, it may be a good thing!'

Body Language

A public speaker is a person – a human being; an intelligent creature – not just a voice. When you make a speech it should come from deep within you and it is the *whole* of you that should project it, so don't rely simply upon your vocal chords to express your feelings: let your whole body communicate your emotions and ideas.

This doesn't mean that you should speak as though you were suffering from St Vitus' Dance. It means you should remember to be reasonably expressive.

Your Face

Your face is the most expressive part of your anatomy. We all know people who can say a thousand words in one look, and without pulling self-consciously funny faces you too can use your face to show how you feel.

If you are telling a funny story and *you* think it is funny, then show it. Smiling is like the measles – it spreads – and a smile on your face will lead to others, like someone who yawns in a railway carriage. A smile is the best way to begin any speech – smile at your audience before you say a word. If you are about to say how pleased you are to be there, then show that you are pleased. Let your smile be relaxed and natural – a forced grimace will have the opposite effect.

When dealing with a serious issue let your emotions show as well. One speaker I know was telling a personal story about a tragic incident in her life to illustrate a point. Halfway through her voice faltered, and she had to pull herself together to be able to carry on. Later she was angry at what had happened. 'I felt such a fool,' she complained, and yet her speech brought an overwhelming response. People really believed in her cause because she felt some emotion and showed it. In a public speech, sincerity will never harm you.

Your Eyes

The eyes have a language of their own which any nationality can understand. Look at people in the street, on a train, their eyes will often tell you what they are thinking. Anger, grief, fear, surprise, hatred and love can all be shown in the eyes, and if someone is insincere it is their eyes that give them away. Don't forget to look at your audience as you speak *and* to look around you. Never stare straight ahead of you, and take care not to keep looking down either. The next time someone says to you, 'Don't look at me in that tone of voice,' you will realize that it is not such a ridiculous remark as it may sound.

Your Head

Your face may be an important feature, but where would it be without your head? Use your head effectively. Heads have a much wider scope than nodding for 'yes' and shaking for 'no'. To illustrate different points, you can throw your head back, bend forward, look round, close your eyes even. Naturally you mustn't overdo it or you will seem eccentric and mannered.

Your Arms

Most of us at some time 'talk' with our hands. If we are describing the shape of some object, we move our arms and hands about to help communication.

Sit down in front of the television when there is a speaker on and turn the volume down. Concentrate on how much he or she uses arms, fingers and hands to express him or herself, and how much you can understand from the gestures alone.

If you watch a mime artist you will know instantly what the gestures mean. Place your palms together and rest the back of one hand against a cheek – sleep! One finger under your right eye – a tear! One hand on each side of your head with the palms pressing against your face – despair! And so you can go on.

Gestures are necessary to make your speech colourful, but the key to making gestures is to *use them in moderation*. Dr Magnus Pyke may have become celebrated for his arm-waving, but there are exceptions to every rule, and ones that are not necessarily to be emulated.

Let your gestures come naturally: don't try to suppress them, but don't overdo them. Begin the gesture *just before* you speak, rather as if you were going to say 'Come here' when you would start to beckon before actually saying the words.

Test all gestures in private before you use them in public. They may feel fine to you but look clumsy when performed. Watch other speakers and see what looks effective, but remember, you and your speech are far more important than your gestures. You are not engaged as an actor to give a performance, but a speaker with something to communicate.

Voice Control

'Let him now speak, or else hereafter forever hold his peace ...'

When speaking in public the last thing it is possible to do is hold your peace. You must engage the interest of your listeners as soon as you begin, and a good speaker who knows how to use his or her voice can make complicated subjects easier to understand.

Your voice, if pleasantly controlled, will form a bond between you and your audience. Remember how often *you* judge people by the way they speak.

But do not be worried about – let alone ashamed of – your accent. Your accent is part of your personality as well as the heritage of your country. Remember too:

1. Timing is important. Do not gabble your speech, but speak slowly and clearly – just a shade slower than in ordinary conversation. This not only helps your listeners but will give you an opportunity to think about what you are going to say next.

2. Don't break up your sentences too much. Pause, but don't break sentences into halves or quarters so that you never say more than four words without pausing. A comfortable speed is 110 words a minute, so check your speed, either by speaking into a tape-recorder for one minute and counting the number of words you used, or by reading aloud from a book for one minute.

3. Modulate your voice to avoid monotony in your delivery. If anything try to speak in a slightly lower pitch than your normal voice. A particularly high voice can be very irritating and difficult to listen to. But do not concentrate on this if it results in artificial speech or draws attention from *what* you are saying. The *what* is always more important than the *how*.

4. Learn to emphasize key words and phrases either by raising your voice slightly, pausing just before giving them full weight, or by lowering the tone of your voice when you want the words to remain firmly in your listeners' minds. With this tactic your audience has to concentrate more and will listen harder. Take care, however, not to let your voice drop at the end of sentences.

5. Speak clearly but without shouting. Shouting at people becomes boring and listeners will be unable to concentrate on what you are saying. Acoustics, of course, vary from place to place, but never shout those immortal words: 'Can you hear me at the back?' Some comedian is more than likely to shout 'No'. It is very amateurish and shows a lack of confidence in yourself and the organization for whom you are speaking. The test to discover whether or not you can be heard at the back of the room is to glance at the faces of the people there when you begin your speech and their expressions will give you a clue as to how well they can hear you.

6. To speak distinctly it is necessary to be aware of each syllable in a word, and to pay special attention to your intonation. Listen to almost any of the news-readers on Radio 4 and the better ones on television. Note how they change the tone and pitch of their voice with each new item, so as to make every announcement fresh and lively.

Voice Exercises

1. Become aware of your tongue, teeth, lips and jaw and test your articulation by getting a friend to listen to you. For example, say:

    'Some others do have them.'

If you say it correctly he will not think you said:

    'Some mothers do have them.'

    Say: 'An ice house.'

If he hears 'A nice house,' you'd better start again.

2. Note the emphasis in sentences, and how the changes in stress patterns can alter the entire meaning of what you have to say. Consider the sentence:

    I know you like your brand new jacket.

Where should the stress be, to make your intentions clear?

    I know you like your brand new jacket (*I* know, but others might not).

    I *know* you like your brand new jacket (gives added assurance that you know).

    I know *you* like your brand new jacket (*you* like it but nobody else does).

    I know you *like* your brand new jacket (well, you like it but that isn't sufficient reason for wearing it on this occasion).

    I know you like *your* brand new jacket (you don't care about anybody else's).

    I know you like your *brand new* jacket (but you don't like any of your old ones).

    I know you like your brand new *jacket* (but you're not keen on the trousers or skirt).

Here we have one simple sentence with the emphasis in seven different places, each giving it an entirely new meaning by changing the weight. Try this with other sentences.

3. Emphasis need not only be placed upon words, but vowels can be emphasized and elongated. Special effects can be made by elongating certain words, so have a go at lengthening vowels. Exaggerated at first like the actresses who call each other 'Daaaaahrling ... '. Then attempt a more controlled version.

'He is far, far too modest ... ' may sound more amusing if you say: 'He is faaar, faaaar too modest ...' and so on.

4. Practise all the vowel sounds first out loud and then put them each into a word.

5. Experiment with the strength and volume of your voice by whispering words and phrases, firstly so that only you can hear.

Then increase the volume so that somebody sitting at the other side of a desk from you can hear.

Then loud enough to fill a small room.

Then loud enough to fill a large hall.

Then as if addressing an audience in the open air.

These exercises will increase your awareness of your vocal capabilities, and help you improve the power and control of your speech.

Nerves

Without nerves nobody ever made a good speech.

Lord Mancroft

Nerves are necessary to a good speaker, and even the most experienced speakers feel nervous before they speak. To try to eliminate nerves altogether would be a mistake, for if controlled properly your nervous energy can be redirected to bring out the best in you. Some people suffer badly from nerves and literally shake all over, but such nerves can be controlled. *Never*, however, try to control them with alcohol or drugs. One drink 'to steady your nerves' could make you rely on it and this could be your undoing.

Nervousness stems from fear – fear that you will be inadequate, that you will make a fool of yourself, that you will dry up, or be misunderstood. With thorough preparation these fears can be eliminated, and you can then use your nervous energy to advantage.

If you have planned your speech carefully, know your subject inside out, made sufficient notes to prompt your memory, you should feel perfectly confident. Once you know the correct techniques of public speaking, you should have nothing to fear.

No concert soloist, for example, would ever attempt to appear on stage if he or she had never played the piece before or practised it sufficiently, and the same applies to you. Know your technique and your material, and you will have nothing to fear.

Worry that you will be misunderstood can only come from inadequate preparation and a lack of knowledge of your subject, which is why it is important only to talk about subjects which you really know thoroughly.

Fear that you will not be heard can be overcome by voice exercises and practice, or improvements in the seating arrangements. The more you practise the better you will become.

You may also have the fear of uncontrollable body reactions. Your mouth becomes dry, your throat tightens up ... what do you do? A dry mouth can be remedied with a sip of water, or if you cannot take a drink just think of sucking a lemon. It may sound silly, but it works.

If your hands and body shake with nerves while you are speaking, concentrate the shakes in your knees. Deliberately try to shift the shaking down your body to your kneecaps. On the way it will probably evaporate. If it doesn't, your trembling knees may well be hidden behind the table or podium.

With experience you will find you won't shake. It will help you not to if, as you stand or as you make your way to the platform, you take some deep breaths, and then pause to calm yourself before you begin to speak.

If possible, try to take a few breaths of fresh air outside – really inhale deeply and hold the air in your lungs for a count of ten before you release it very slowly. This will increase the oxygen in your blood, and help you think more calmly and clearly.

If 'nerves' are a major problem for you, it will be worth doing some relaxation exercises well before your speech.

Neck

A lot of tension builds up in the neck, so rotate your head round in a circular motion slowly, beginning by resting your chin on your chest and rolling your head around to the right until your right ear brushes past your right shoulder; then round and back as far as your head will go (as if you were trying to get the top of your head in between your shoulder blades); and round so that your left ear brushes past your left shoulder as your head comes round to its original position. Do this two or three times, and then repeat, moving your head in the opposite direction.

Face

Screw up your face tightly. Screw up your eyes, wrinkle your nose and purse your lips as if you were going to give someone a big kiss. Then let all the muscles in your face relax. It might be a good idea to do this exercise in the privacy of the cloakroom before you make your speech, and certainly *never* while making your speech!

Body

There are numerous exercises designed to relax your body and these four are personal favourites. Do them at home before setting out to make the speech, or even a few weeks beforehand if just the thought of it gives you the jitters.

1. Lie down on the floor, flat on your back with the palms of your hands facing upwards. Close your eyes and relax. Tense all the muscles in your toes as tightly as you can. Hold for a count of five. Let them relax. Tense your foot muscles. Push down with your heels. Hold for a count of five. Then relax. Work systematically through every muscle of your body – not forgetting your shoulders, face, even your scalp. Tense each muscle in turn and after a hold of about five seconds, let the muscle relax. By the time you reach the end of this exercise, your limbs will feel really heavy and you will be completely relaxed.

2. Take a warm shower and let the water spray on to your limbs and run down your body. The sensation is particularly relaxing, and is one that you should try to *imagine* at times when you need to relax.

3. Sit down and imagine that you are made of stone. Having sat perfectly still for a few minutes, imagine that a warm liquid is flowing soothingly into your feet. Enjoy the warm sensation as the liquid flows up your legs and throughout your entire body until you are a mass of flowing liquid.

4. Lie back on the floor with your head on a pillow and the soles of your feet on the floor. Push down with your feet and head and raise the rest of your body into an arch, just as if you had a rope around your middle and someone was trying to pull you up, but your feet and head are stuck to the floor. Hold this position as long as you can and then collapse into a heap and enjoy this relaxation.

Warning: Do not move around too quickly after relaxation exercises. Approach with care and stop if there is any discomfort.

Rehearsal

Sir Winston Churchill used to rehearse his speeches in the bath, and on one occasion Sir Winston's valet thought he heard the great man calling him so he entered the bathroom, and asked if his assistance was required. 'No,' growled Churchill, 'I wasn't talking to you, I was addressing the House of Commons.'

Rehearse your own speeches in the bath, by all means, and try them out on your family as well. The more you practise the more confident you will feel, and the more confident you feel the more relaxed your eventual performance will be.

It is only when you are in complete command of yourself and your material that your speech will seem spontaneous. Appearing to speak effortlessly is hard work. Looking relaxed is nerve-racking. But sitting down with the sound of tumultuous applause echoing in your ears is wonderfully satisfying – so keep at it!

3

OPENING AND CLOSING
YOUR SPEECH

Oratory is just like prostitution: you must have little tricks.
                                    Victorio Emanuel Orlando

Methods of Opening
Sir Thomas Beecham, talking about an orchestra, once
remarked that 'the great thing is to begin together and end
together, what happens in between doesn't matter very much'.
The same sentiment could apply when it comes to public
speaking. Of course, Sir Thomas was speaking with his tongue in
his cheek, because it is unlikely that he would have
countenanced an unharmonious middle, any more than you
would want the heart of your speech to be discordant.

A good opening and closing are nevertheless essential, and
most speakers formulate the two together so that they tie up.
This is a good idea, just so long as they are relevant to the main
body of your speech.

The opening should arouse your audience's interest, and it is
your job to see that it does. If you decide upon a humorous
introduction, or even an element of surprise for starters, do allow
it to have some relevance to your theme, and lead you smoothly
into it.

As already mentioned, the aim of your opening is to grab the
attention of your audience, to whet their appetite so that they
are eager for more. It is easier to hold their attention than to gain
it half way through your speech. Although there are limits to the
number of ways to begin a speech, the 'tried and trusted'

methods are usually the best. The *methods*, that is, not the words.

The words should be your own, so *never* begin with 'Unaccustomed as I am to public speaking ...' *or* 'A funny thing happened on my way here tonight ...'

1. *Humorous openings.* Although effective, and likely to project an image of you as a friendly person, there are dangers involved in a humorous start.

Unless you are known to your audience as a humorist, or a 'card', they may not realize that your opening remark is intended to be funny. They may still be 'settling down' and may miss the point of your opening quip – especially if it isn't strictly relevant.

If you *are* going to begin with a joke, don't, for example, say: 'A friend of mine recently bumped his head and was advised to rub brandy on the bump. I saw him two days later and asked him if the brandy was working.

' "I don't know," he replied, "I never seem to be able to get the glass past my mouth."

'Well, tonight we've had some excellent brandy, but now we come to the best part of the evening ...'

The joke has absolutely nothing to do with the subject of your speech and really is a pointless way to begin.

But suppose you are going to talk about the misuse of the English language, to begin with a relevant joke would be acceptable:

'This morning I was in a bookshop in Charing Cross Road, when a smartly dressed man came in and asked if they had a copy of *Omar Khayyam*.

' "Sorry, sir," said the girl, "we 'ave 'is *Illiad* and 'is *Hodessey* but not 'is *Khayyam*."

'Now this made me think very seriously about the decline in the language once known as the Queen's English ...'

2. *Starting with a question.* This can stimulate your listeners' interest and get them thinking. You may have a serious and important point to make, and a challenging opening question may be the simplest and most effective way of leading up to it:

'Our prisons are already overcrowded. There is no more money available to spend on them. Crime is increasing – dramatically. Ladies and gentlemen, this is an alarming situation. What are we going to do about it?'

Having put your question, pause for a moment while your audience absorbs what you have asked them, and then begin to answer the question yourself.

An opening question can work equally if you are planning a more light-hearted approach:

'Did you know that over 100,000 people die every year by gas? Twenty-five per cent were burnt because of it, twenty per cent inhaled it, and fifty-five per cent stepped on it.'

A question provides a neat – but not contrived – way of introducing your subject, and intriguing your audience.

3. *Hard-hitting statements*. A short and powerful sentence that will lead you into your main theme can be very effective and a bit like punching your listener between the eyes if you really want to stun him. This single sentence is used to its best advantage when you are making a particularly serious speech.

On the centenary of Voltaire's death, Victor Hugo delivered an emotional and fitting tribute to the great philosopher. He began with these stirring words: 'A hundred years today a man died. He died immortal.'

In 1946 Bernard M. Baruch made a very different kind of speech about the control of atomic weapons. This is how he began:

'We are here to make a choice between the quick and the dead. That is our business.

'Behind the black portent of the new atomic age lies a hope which, seized upon with faith, can work our salvation. If we fail, then we have damned every man to be the slave of fear. Let us not deceive ourselves: we must elect world peace or world destruction.'

No one could fail to sit up and take notice after that.

So often a simple and direct statement of fact proves to be the most effective approach.

Recently, when I was asked to propose a toast to The Ladies, I thought I would try to combine all three opening gambits – being humorous, asking a question, and making a startling statement of fact, all at the same time. I rose to my feet and began: 'Gentlemen – and ladies – did you know that Queen Marie Antoinette and Jayne Mansfield shared identical bust measurements?'

4. *Quotations and poems.* Whatever the occasion a relevant quotation can be effectively used to begin your speech. But be ruthless in your choice so that its relevance is clear and it allows you to follow straight in to your main subject.

You can begin: 'An old French proverb says "Life is half spent before one knows what life is". And how true that is ...'

Or you can start with the quote itself: ' "We are born crying, live complaining and die disappointed." That rather cynical view of life appeared in an eighteenth-century book by a doctor called Thomas Fuller ...'

Always give credit for the quotation, however, and don't simply begin, 'Life is made up of marble and mud ...' Someone in the audience will know the origin of the quotation and dub you a plagiarist.

Poetry too can be used in a similar manner to start your speech. Perhaps you are going to give a tongue-in-cheek speech about women drivers, so you could begin:

Mary had a little car,
She drove in manner deft.
But every time she signalled right,
The little car turned left.

Or a speech about pessimism:

'Twixt the optimist and the pessimist
The difference is droll.
The optimist sees the doughnut
While the pessimist sees the hole.

Even a more serious speech can begin with a light verse. I

recently attended a dinner at which a chief constable opened his address on Crime Prevention in the 1980s with this short poem:

> The rain it raineth on the just,
> And also on the unjust fella;
> But chiefly on the just, because,
> The unjust steals the just's umbrella.

The main point to remember when using poetry is to *keep it short*. Too long a piece will lose the listeners' concentration. Remember too that a piece that rhymes will be easier on the ears and will usually be more appreciated.

5. *Personal openings*. A personal opening should express your feelings at giving the speech. Perhaps as chairperson of the Women's Rowing Club you feel honoured to represent such a body of enthusiastic and fun-loving women, so say so. At any function you may feel it an honour to have been asked to speak, so give your reasons why and explain what you have to offer.

Despite your natural modesty, avoid saying you can't think why you were asked to speak. It shows a lack of confidence, and if you are very unlucky somebody might just say: 'All the other people we wanted were otherwise engaged tonight!'

Try to avoid unintentional slips if possible. A distinguished lady of my acquaintance truly didn't realize what she was saying when she began an after-dinner speech in a Devon hotel in front of 250 guests, with the immortal words: 'I can't tell you what a great pleasure and honour it is for you to have me here this evening ... '

6. *The stunt*. Some experienced speakers begin their speech with a stunt, such as tearing up their prepared speech after the first line or even setting fire to it, bursting a blown-up paper bag to wake up the audience, or saying something like:

'Underneath one chair tonight is Sellotaped the number 623. Will you all stand up and see if it's under your chair. The winner will get this magnum of champagne.' After everyone has stood up the speaker either finds the number under *his* chair, or says: 'Oh, sorry. It's next week at the Senior Citizens' Club – I got the wrong week ...' etc.

Stunts are not recommended for the inexperienced speaker, but are useful to one who happens to be eleventh on a list of twelve speakers, and needs something to liven up the proceedings.

Methods of Closing

As the song says:

It's not how you start it's how you finish,
It's not how you begin, it's how you end ...

Well, that's very much how it is with public speaking. It's no good starting with a big rousing opening if by the end you are battling against the snores or the scraping chairs to make yourself heard.

Your ending is important because that is the memory of you that the audience will take home with them and if you end with a laugh, a heart-stirring sentiment, or a thought-provoking remark – that (if anything) is what the audience will be thinking about on their way home.

Here are the memorable closing lines of speeches by three public figures of this century.

Douglas MacArthur: 'And like the old soldier of that ballad, I now close my military career and just fade away, an old soldier who tried to do his duty as God gave him the light to see that duty.'

Neville Chamberlain: ' ... I am too much of a realist to believe that we are going to achieve our purpose in a day. We have only laid the foundations of peace. The superstructure is not even begun.'

Richard Nixon: ' ... Our destiny offers not the cup of despair, but the chalice of opportunity. So let us seize it, not in fear, but in gladness – and "riders on the earth together", let us go forward, firm in our faith, steadfast in our purpose, cautious of the dangers: but sustained by our confidence in the will of God and the promise of man.'

Now whatever you happen to think of the three individuals

(and isn't hindsight a wonderful thing?) those endings leave no doubt in the mind as to the feelings and position of each speaker and give the listener much food for thought, which all good speeches should do.

The worst possible endings to any speech would be to say: 'Well, that's all.' 'Thanks for listening to me.' 'Right. That's it. Thank you.'

Try to have a *purpose* to your ending. It is just as much part of the speech as the main body. As one eminent speaker once put it, 'A tail isn't just there to nearly end off a dog, it is there for a reason.'

1. *Food for thought*. The endings to speeches I have just quoted were heart-stirring and left a message. Appealing to the listeners' conscience is also often effective, for instance: ' … and I think if we all pull together, we can't help but succeed in the end. What do *you* think?'

Here you have left the audience with a question in their minds that should make them think about the points you have raised.

2. *Quotations*. As with an opening, a relevant quotation often makes a good finale, but don't use one for the beginning *and* the end. If you have a special message in your speech then a quotation that emphasizes your main point could be used, as in the following closing lines from a speech by oliver Wendell Holmes:

'And so I end with a line from a Latin poet who uttered the message more than fifteen hundred years ago, "Death plucks my ear and says: live – I am coming." '

In 1977 Margaret Thatcher gave a speech on The New Renaissance, in Zurich, and successfully ended her speech with a piece of poetry:

'The new renaissance of which I spoke was perhaps best described by Kipling:

So when the world is asleep, and there seems no hope of waking,
Out of some long, bad dream that makes her mutter and moan,

Suddenly, all men arise to the noise of fetter breaking,
And everyone smiles at his neighbour and tells him his soul
is his own.'

Winston Churchill was another politician who ended some of
his speeches successfully with poetry. Obviously if using poetry
or a quotation, do make quite certain that it is appropriate.

3. *Anecdotes and stories.* If using an anecdote or story it must
contain your message, perhaps pointing out a particular moral,
or a lesson which you yourself have had passed on to you.

If you are paying a tribute to a particular person, or speaking
at a dinner in honour of someone, then a touching anecdote that
brings out their best qualities will certainly be appreciated.

4. *Humorous endings.* Here you must be absolutely certain of
your material. Ending with a joke is a risky business and
certainly not for the uninitiated. Nothing would be more
humiliating than to end on a joke that fell flat. A joke, as always,
must be relevant. Don't simply end by saying:

'As the girl said when she finished cutting the lawn with nail
scissors: "That's all there is, there isn't any mower." '

Such an ending would seem as if you simply couldn't think of
anything better to say, and as much effort must be put into your
ending as in the whole speech, which is why some professional
speakers work out a really good ending first, and then devise
their speech around it.

As Browning says: 'What began best can't end worst.'

If you want a humorous ending, it is probably safer to go for
'gentle' humour rather than a belly-laugh. Try to keep it light and
you will not go far wrong.

As an example of 'gentle' humour, here is a story I heard
recounted at a dinner recently. The speaker's theme was Famous
last Words:

'When Lord Holland was on his deathbed, his friend and rival
George Selwyn called to inquire how his Lordship was and left
his card. This was taken to Lord Holland who said: "If Mr
Selwyn calls again, show him into my room. If I am alive I shall

be glad to see him. If I am dead I am sure he will be delighted to see me." '

5. *The stunt.* A surprise ending can work, but isn't recommended for the inexperienced. Some speakers get themselves a standing ovation by cleverly performing a stunt which obliges the audience to stand up! Bruce Forsyth sometimes asks if he can take a photograph of his audience for his poor aged mother, and gets them standing to applaud, while he produces his Instamatic.

Such an ending is certainly different and gets you noticed, but as a rule beware of gimmicks. They are usually something to fall back on when you haven't got anything good to say!

'A speech is like a love affair. Any fool can start it, but to end it requires considerable skill.' So said Lord Mancroft, one of Britain's most brilliant after-dinner speakers. He is someone who never needs to resort to gimmicks. (Unfortunately, there are times when I do. When desperate – i.e. when I feel my final sally has fallen flat – at the end of my speech, I don't sit down: I stand on my head. Yes, it's true. I put my head on the table and swing my legs up into the air – and stay there until the audience has burst into amazed applause.)

However, you choose to end, never forget the importance of that last impression. Try to keep your ending short and don't bring in any new information. Come what may, do your best to be original. Anyone can end with 'all that remains for me to say … ' etc., but you don't want your audience thinking you're just 'anyone'.

What we want is a story that begins with an earthquake and works its way up to a climax.
                                             Samuel Goldwyn

4

SPEECHES FOR ALL OCCASIONS

Every speech you make should be tailored to the occasion. Obviously (or, anyway, hopefully) the speech you make at the annual sales conference is going to be different from the speech you make as the father of the bride. For the speech-maker, each type of occasion has special requirements – and pitfalls.

After-Dinner Speeches

Someone once said that the art of after-dinner speaking is to dilute a two-minute idea with a two-hour vocabulary. Nothing could be further from the truth. I believe the secret of successful after-dinner speaking can be summed up in three words: Preparation, Wit, Brevity.

Preparation is essential. With it you will be able to give the impression of spontaneity. Genuine spontaneity can be useful too! Prince Philip is a seasoned speaker who is invariably well prepared, but at his most effective when spicing his prepared speech with additional off-the-cuff remarks.

Take the memorable occasion when he was made a fellow of the Royal College of Surgeons. At the ceremony he was presented with a small silver cup with the words: 'May it please your Highness to accept this Bleeding Cup!' to which Prince Philip replied, 'I can only say it is bloody kind of you!'

After dinner, wit is essential too. The after-dinner speaker is there to amuse his audience, not to lecture or moralize. As Lord Boothby, one of the best after-dinner speakers of his generation, put it: 'We are there to entertain. To give the party a sense of

well-being, to make it an occasion, or to make asses of ourselves.
It is up to us to see that we don't do the latter.'

As we all know, brevity really is the soul of wit, so as soon as
you are asked to make an after-dinner speech find out exactly
how long you will be expected to talk for – and don't exceed your
time limit by so much as thirty seconds. You don't want to be the
one of whom it is said, 'He has a marvellous knack of packing a
five minute speech into half an hour.'

Conventions and Conference Speeches

One of the most difficult kinds of speech to make is one at a
business convention or conference that lasts for several days. If
you speak on the first day your colleagues will be fresh and eager
to listen, but imagine the challenge of having the dubious
'honour' of speaking on the final day of a week-long conference.

In the United States they have a special prayer for convention
speakers:

'God bless the speakers on the first day of the convention. May
their listeners be eager and ready to hear what they have to say,
and give full support and consideration to their ideas.

'God bless the speakers on the second day, give them the
strength and power to pass any mental blocks and stimulate the
minds of the weary and disillusioned.

'And to the speaker on the last day of the convention – may
God have mercy on his soul.'

The art of organizing a successful conference deserves a book
to itself (and there are several good ones), but if you are
organizing a conference yourself you can make it easier for the
speakers with sensible planning. Devote each day – if not each
hour – of the conference to a fresh subject so that the listeners do
not get stale. If possible, save a popular lively topic for the end to
help ensure enthusiasm throughout. The cliché holds true: save
the best till last!

If you find yourself speaking at the end of a conference and
your listeners *are* weary, do not despair. The way to look at it is
as a challenge, and if you handle it well you will actually have an
advantage over other speakers. Remember that the end of your

speech is what leaves a lasting impression on your audience. This can apply to conference speaking as well. Do it cleverly and your speech will stick in people's minds when the speeches of those who opened the conference have long been forgotten.

Throughout the conference listen carefully to the speeches of others. You want people to listen to you, so it is courtesy to listen to them. But you know the content of their speeches before you make yours which gives you a definite advantage. Make a note of the main points in other speeches and compare them with yours.

See which points you agree with, which you don't like and where the ideas can be improved upon. Use what you have learnt when preparing your speech. That doesn't mean you should adopt the ideas of others, but it will show that you are aware of what has gone before. All too many convention and conference speakers deliver a set-piece address prepared weeks in advance. The successful conference speaker delivers a speech that is a *part* of the conference, that relates to what has gone before and is obviously the work of someone who keeps his ears, his eyes and his mind open.

When you are speaking at a conference where you are there to *sell* something, never forget that before you sell your product, you've got to sell yourself. Be enthusiastic (enthusiasm is catching), be truthful (trustworthiness is essential in a salesman) and give your potential customers what you believe they want to hear.

As Will Rogers put it: 'If you go fishing you bait the hook, not with what you like, but what the fish likes.'

Introductory Speeches
Even if a speaker is so famous that he 'needs no introduction' you will find that before he can rise to make his speech, he *does* need an introduction.

It can and should be brief and to the point, but at the same time welcoming and informative. If the speaker you are introducing has a set theme, then this is the pattern your introduction should follow:

Step 1: Introduce the subject.

Step 2: Stress importance to the audience.

Step 3: Qualify the speaker.

By discussing the subject to be spoken of first, you whet the appetite of the audience, and at the same time boost the ego of the speaker who feels it his duty and honour now to give this speech. By stressing the importance of the subject to the audience you turn the event into an occasion, because it makes them feel as if something special is going to happen.

By then producing an 'expert' and leading authority on this particular subject, you have built your introductory speech into a fitting climax, and the audience will be applauding as the speaker takes his position, and you will have set the atmosphere.

Avoid telling jokes when introducing a speaker, that is not your task on this occasion, and it is both unfair and discourteous to attempt to steal his thunder.

Here is a straightforward introduction, based on one I heard recently. It isn't very exciting, but it serves its purpose and satisfactorily introduces Dr Jonathan Jones, authority on lead pollution, to members of the Fresh Air Society:

'Friends of the Fresh Air Society, and honoured guests. It would seem that every leap forward for mankind has its attendant hazards. Nobody can deny that the internal combustion engine has brought enormous benefits to mankind – but at a price. Pollution.

'Lead in particular is a hazard of which our grandparents were blissfully ignorant – but which it behoves us to tackle vigorously if we are to avoid its truly alarming effects. Our children – the future citizens of our country – are the ones most at risk, since they are taking in lead poison with the very air they breathe.

'Dr Jonathan Jones has spent the last five years studying pollution in general, and lead pollution in particular. And here to enlighten us on this vital and topical danger, is Dr Jonathan Jones.'

That very straightforward introduction included all the essential details; it introduced the subject, it involved the listeners, and it introduced the speaker. That is all any introduction should do. If you, as chairperson, do happen to know the speaker personally and have had a long association, then you might like to begin with a personal anecdote – and even a modest joke – so long as you keep it short:

'Thirty years ago I had the pleasure of introducing a young and very polished speaker who showed quite early that age has no barriers when it comes to communication. On that occasion an unexploded landmine chose to go off a few streets away, and undaunted he continued with his speech. Since that time he has become one of the country's best-loved speakers and always goes down a bomb! It gives me enormous pleasure to introduce you to Bosco Hoggins.'

Finally, do remember to check with your speaker beforehand if you intend to make any announcement or comment on the subject of his speech. He may want it to remain a surprise, or you could cause embarrassment if you introduce him as one of the country's funniest speakers, when he intends to give a serious speech.

And whatever you do, pronounce his name correctly. This is a plea from the heart. Gyles Brandreth is tired of being introduced as Charles Brantub.

Impromptu Speeches

As a general rule it is not advisable to indulge in extempore speeches if you do not have an opportunity to prepare material. Some people can speak very well at the drop of a hat and completely unrehearsed, but unless you are a Peter Ustinov such speeches tend to lack the polish and fluency that adequate preparation ensures.

Planning allows you to revise your speech until you are completely happy with it and helps relieve any nerves and gives added confidence.

The only time that you are going to be suddenly called upon to make an impromptu speech of this kind is in the case of a surprise, perhaps a surprise party or presentation, or in the case of an emergency, in which case nobody is going to expect a long and eloquent oration.

Whatever the reason for making the impromptu speech come

straight to the point and say exactly what you feel. Don't say 'I don't know what to say', but let the emotion of the moment speak for you. Often the spontaneity of the occasion will enable you to make an excellent short speech.

Try to eliminate 'ers' and 'ums' and take care not to waffle. If you feel an 'er' or an 'um' coming on, try to replace it with a pause. Speakers can waffle even in prepared speeches so pay particular attention with an impromptu one. I heard a speaker once who began:

'Henry the Eighth was a fat man. Very fat. He was really quite stout and large in stature, and certainly by no stretch of the imagination a slim man ...'

Do not speak just for the sake of it when forced into making an impromptu speech – be sincere but concise.

Kindred Speeches
In theory a speech that you make in front of your family and friends should be the easiest of all, and yet some people (like me) would rather speak in front of 200 strangers whom they may never see again, than risk making a fool of themselves in front of 20 relatives.

To most of us family gatherings are for a special occasion: the 21st birthday celebrations, the silver wedding, the engagement party, Christmas festivities, and even great-grandma's 100th birthday – all to be remembered for years to come ... and with a bit of luck, treasured.

Whatever the occasion a speech makes it that extra bit special, if for no other reason than that it provides you with an opportunity to say the things you would like to say at other times, but never do. You may find it hard to say how much you appreciate your parents, for example, and so you never say it, but a speech provides you with the golden chance.

Give just as much thought to this 'family' speech as you would to a major 'public' speech, and do say only *good* things. All right, you can't stand Auntie Flo and Uncle Arthur, but this is not the time to air your grievances or cause family strife, so tread carefully.

In his play *Heartbreak House* Bernard Shaw wrote: 'When our relatives are at home, we have to think of all their good points or it would be impossible to endure them.'

That thought should be borne in mind. The family speech is one occasion when you can really go to town with your speech – jokes, stories, quotes, anecdotes (especially family memories), always go down well with loving parents and grandparents, and although you will probably not wish to speak for long anyway, there is less need for a strict time limit and they won't be afraid to chivvy you if you go on too long: 'Come on, son, the trifle's getting cold!' 'Get on with it, Dad, we're going on holiday in July!'

If you do feel embarrassed about making a speech in front of your family and do not know what to say, keep it very *very* simple and one hundred per cent sincere. This is a verbatim transcription of a speech delivered by the son of friends of mine on his eighteenth birthday. It could hardly have been more elementary – or more effective.

'Mum and Dad, Gran and Grandad, everyone. It's not every day that a person comes of age, and today is one that I have looked forward to for a very long time. Thanks to all of you here it really has turned into a very happy and memorable day that I shall cherish. I would like to say a very special thank you to Mum and Dad for all their love and devotion over the years. I know I haven't always shown my appreciation, but you've always supported me and I hope to be worthy of you in the future.

'Thanks to all of you too for your wonderful gifts and for giving me such a lovely party this evening. There aren't words to express how I feel at the moment, except that I'm very very happy and it's all thanks to you. Perhaps we can all raise our glasses and drink a toast to the future. Here's to all of us.'

Opening Functions

If you are going to officially 'open' a particular function, be it a garden fête, a Christmas bazaar, or a charity sale, brevity is essential, because frequently your audience is standing, there are children who have to be kept quiet, stalls itching to take money, latecomers arriving, and so on.

On such occasions five minutes is the outside limit, so

organization is required to say what you have to say in the allotted time. Having your main points jotted on a postcard should help keep you on the track.

1. Begin by thanking whoever has introduced you. It might be the chairman or president of an association, so find out his or her name beforehand.

2. If there has been a particular reason for your having been asked, perhaps because of personal associations with the town or a particular interest in the charity or organization, continue by giving your reasons for wanting to attend. A well-chosen anecdote could be included here.

3. Say exactly *who* will benefit from the occasion financially – whether it is to go to Action Research for the Crippled Child, the National Playing Fields Association, the Church Steeple Fund, or whatever – and justify the charity concerned. Give brief examples of the valuable work that the charity does.

4. Thank the organizers for the work in arranging the function. Encourage people to spend money.

5. Officially declare the function open.

Follow this basic structure when preparing any kind of 'opening' speech. Even if you are opening a new motorway or bridge, point 3 can still apply as you can talk about the benefits that this new structuire will inevitably bring and encourage people to use it.

Presentation Speeches
If ever you are called upon to make a presentation you will find that only four things need to be done in your speech:

1. State the origin of the award: 'Each year the Lemon Aid Society award the Stanley Bilbo Memorial Trophy in honour of its founder.'

2. Give the reason for its presentation: 'This beautiful cup is presented to the member of the Society who has, in the opinion of the committee, during the past twelve months, made the greatest contribution to the Welfare of Lemons in this country.'

3. Reveal what the person did to merit the award: 'Drucilla Farmer has worked tirelessly and with total commitment to increase the public's awareness of our aims and has raised over one million pounds in the last three years for the cause. Because of her unfailing devotion she has been selected by the committee to receive this trophy to mark her outstanding achievement.'

4. Present the award: 'It now gives me very great pleasure to present you, Drucilla, with this giant lemon. Many congratulations.'

If you are going to a function at which you think you might be receiving an award, it's as well to be prepared. Even if in the event someone else is presented with the award, it is best to plan what to say 'just in case'. Nobody expects a long speech on such occasions, and it is one instance where a long speech is considered to be in particularly poor taste. This is all you need to do:

1. Thank the person who has given you the award: 'Thank you, Mr President, for your kind words and for giving me this beautiful lemon.'

2. Show your gratitude to the organization behind the award: 'I am deeply grateful to the Society for honouring me like this. The Society has always been close to my heart and I shall treasure this award always.'

3. Say what you will do with the award: 'I intend to stand the lemon on my desk so that as I work I shall be reminded of all of you! Thank you.'

Nothing could be simpler, and the three basic steps can be used and adapted to suit any speech of this kind – and it is one that you can prepare at a moment's notice. *Never*, however, make a 'suicide speech' and say that you do not deserve the award or cannot think why you have been given it. It almost certainly isn't true – and even if it is, nobody will believe you!

Leaving and Retirement Speeches

If the presentation is to mark the occasion of your retirement or is a farewell presentation as you leave your job to take up a new position, then the above format still applies. But you might like to include a special word of thanks to managerial staff and colleagues for their help and friendship over the years, and possibly include a personal anecdote or a memory of the company when you first joined twenty-four years ago. Say how you will miss the friends you've made, and what you intend to do in your retirement. Nothing more need be said.

School Speech Days

At school I was a reasonably conscientious pupil and on Speech Day I did my best to endure the proceedings without complaint. Invariably there was the headmaster's annual report, the chairman of the Governors' speech, and a 'few words' from a 'celebrated' ex-pupil.

One year I timed the speeches and noted the times on the programme.

Introduction by the chairman of the Governors	7 minutes
Report by the headmaster	45 minutes
Distribution of prizes and address by ex-pupil, A.N. Nonymous Esq.	38 minutes
Vote of thanks to A.N. Nonymous Esq.	5 minutes
Cheers led by the senior prefect	30 seconds
'God save the Queen'	

Having sat through that little lot there is little wonder we considered Speech Day the most boring day of the year.

If some day you become a 'celebrated ex-pupil' (or even a headmaster) you may be called upon to perform on Speech Day.

Bear in mind what it felt like to be in the audience when you were a child and make your words few and entertaining. Do not be tempted to think 'I suffered when I was here, so why shouldn't these blighters suffer too.'

Keep your speech lively, use jokes and anecdotes providing they are uncomplicated. I seem to remember a speaker at my school rambling on and on with an over-complicated story about a man leaving a factory each day with a wheelbarrow full of sand. Each day the sand was searched as he left to make sure that he was not stealing anything from the factory, but nothing was ever found. The punch line was delivered a good ten minutes after the story started, and was to the effect that what the man was stealing was wheelbarrows! By this time everyone was laughing, but not at the hapless speaker's *joke*. They were laughing at the speaker's foolishness in telling such a long-winded story which had nothing to do with his speech.

As always, only use material that has some bearing upon what you are saying. Use jokes and anecdotes by all means, but make them relevant. On such occasions a little light-hearted nostalgia is perfectly in order.

' ... As I look around this hall today I can't tell you what memories come flooding back. When I was a pupil here I hated French and we had a teacher, who has since retired, whom we used to call "Isaiah", because he had one eye higher than the other. He was an absolute stickler for neatness in dress and he couldn't bear to see anybody lounging around or leaning on walls. One day "Isaiah" walked into the vestibule near the headmaster's office and there a young lad was leaning up against the radiator warming his behind. That was it. "Isaiah" strode across the hall, clipped the boy across the ear, shook him by the shoulders and shouted: "And whose class are you from?"

' "Please, sir," said the lad, "I'm not from any class. I've just come to deliver this parcel from W.H. Smiths."

'French lessons were never the same after that, because every time he came in we would tell him there was a parcel from W.H. Smiths downstairs for him! It was worth getting detention for ...'

Be lively, witty, short and demonstrate that you have something in common with your audience. Never talk down to them, especially when they are children.

The headmaster making his annual report should avoid giving a blow by blow account of the school year, and concentrate on the 'edited highlights': the success of the school play, the winning of the inter-schools badminton championship, the orchestra's tour of Europe. We used to cringe as our headmaster said: ' ... and then at the beginning of March ... ' thinking, 'Good Lord, he's got another nine months to get through yet.'

Toasts
Toasts fall into two categories: loyal and patriotic toasts; and social toasts.

Loyal and Patriotic Toasts
The simplest of all toasts, for no speech is required and the chairman or toastmaster should simply say: 'The Queen'. If he is determined to say more, the most he should say is 'The Queen, God bless her.'

If a second loyal toast is proposed it should be to other members of the royal family; it should follow the first, and once again no speech is required.

Patriotic toasts are usually given at dinners that are directly connected with the Armed Forces. The toast can be: 'Her Majesty's Forces', or it might be given as just one of the forces: either 'The Royal Navy', or 'The Army', or 'The Royal Air Force.'

It is possible for the chairman to give the toast to Her Majesty's Forces, and then one member of each to reply on behalf of their force. In each of the above cases, a very short speech will be required *before* the toast.

With patriotic toasts the motto is: 'Be brief, be sincere, be seated'.

Social Toasts
Social toasts, as the name implies, are toasts proposed at social gatherings, be they weddings, christenings, birthday parties, retirement parties, or what have you.

On such occasions the speeches preceeding the toasts can be longer and more light-hearted:

'Ladies and gentlemen and friends. As a close friend of Alfred and Enid for many years it has given me great joy to celebrate with them the occasion of their Silver Wedding anniversary. All marriage is based on 'give-and-take' – and Alfred said he gives and Enid takes – and no marriage is ever without its arguments and ups and downs – which is why Enid constantly has a rolling-pin in her handbag!

'To talk of a perfect marriage sounds too sentimental but to me this couple here have been perfect friends for all of their twenty-five years together. I would like you to raise your glasses and join me now in wishing them health and happiness over the *next* twenty-five years. Here's to Alfred and Enid.'

On the whole, I believe the speech prior to the actual toast should last no more than two minutes. And the speech should be designed to lead up to the toast itself, which may be specific – 'To Betty and Philip' – or general – 'To absent friends'.

As I have said, I am against the use of jokes and stories culled from books. However, a really apt quotation judiciously used is a different matter. The same goes for quotable toasts, so long as they are sufficiently concise and one hundred per cent relevant. Over the years I have collected such toasts and among the many I have come across – some humorous, some sentimental, some very simple – these are the ones I remember working best:

May we never have friends who, like shadows, keep close to us in the sunshine, only to desert us on a cloudy day.

Here's to our sweethearts and wives;
May our sweethearts soon become our wives,
And our wives ever remain our sweethearts.

May every man become what he thinks himself to be.

May Dame Fortune ever smile on you; but never her daughter – Miss Fortune.

May the right person say the right thing to the right person, in the right way, at the right time, in the right place.

Here's love to one, friendship to a few, and goodwill to all.

To our guest: a friend of our friend's is doubly our friend. Here's to him.

To our hosts: happiness, health and prosperity.

Here's to our home, where a world of strife is shut out and a world of love is shut in.

To the land we live in, love and would die for.

Here's to our absent friends, God bless them.

May the Lord love us but not call us too soon.

To your good health, old friend, may you live for a thousand years, and I be there to count them.

May your joys be as deep as the ocean and your sorrows as light as its foam.

Drink not to my past, which is weak and indefensible,
Nor to my present, which is not above reproach:
But let us drink to our futures, which, thank God, are immaculate.

Here's wishing you the kind of troubles that will last as long as your New Year's resolutions!

Here's to the lasses we've loved, my lad,
Here's to the lips we've pressed;
For of kisses and lasses
Like liquor in glasses,
The last is always the best.

Here's to the bride that is to be,
Happy and smiling and fair,

Here's to those who would like to be
And wondering when and where.

May I present you to a person who knows all there is to know
about banks except breaking and entering.

Here's champagne to our real friends, and real pain to our
sham friends.

Drink! for you know not whence you come, nor why:
Drink! for you know not why you go, nor where.

Here's to matrimony, the high sea for which no compass has
yet been invented.

Here's to the red of the holly berry.
And to its leaf so green;
And here's to the lips that are just as red;
And the fellow who's not so green.

The Ladies – we admire them for their beauty, respect them
for their intelligence, adore them for their virtue, and love them
because we can't help it.

May friendship, like wine, improve as time advances, and may
we always have old wine, old friends, and young cares.

My favourite toasts were both proposed by Mark Twain. The
first, proposed in 1882, was to babies!

'Babies! Now, that's something like. We haven't all had the
good fortune to be ladies; we have not all been generals, or poets,
or statesmen; but when the toast works down to the babies, we
all stand on common ground – for we've all been babies.

'It is a shame that for a thousand years the world's banquets
have utterly ignored the baby, as if he didn't amount to
anything! If you, gentlemen, will stop and think a minute – if
you will go back fifty or a hundred years, to your early married
life and recontemplate your first baby – you will remember that

he amounted to a good deal – and even something over.

'Mr Chairman, gentlemen, I give you Babies!'

This final toast is another of Mark Twain's:

'Let us toast the fools. But for them the rest of us could not succeed.'

Votes of Thanks

When giving a vote of thanks to a speaker, try to include some of the major points that he or she has made, to show that the remarks have been appreciated and absorbed.

A vote of thanks is difficult to prepare in advance because spontaneity is of the essence. The vote of thanks will be a failure – and patently unfelt – if it sounds as though it was prepared weeks prior to the occasion.

If you have been asked to give a vote of thanks, you have *not* been asked to make a speech. Nor have you been asked to attempt to cap the speaker's jokes with some gems of your own, let alone correct his errors of fact with your own superior knowledge. You have been asked to get up, to show that you listened to what the speaker has said, and have enjoyed it, and to thank him or her as warmly as possible.

Don't overdo the praise unless the speech really has been brilliant. To declare it 'the finest speech I have ever heard' when it was, in truth, inarticulate, inaccurate or mediocre, is to lay yourself open to mockery and to rub salt into the wounds of the speaker who will know, deep down, that it wasn't that marvellous. When thanking a poor speaker, be as generous as honesty allows and as brief as courtesy permits.

Wedding Speeches

When you are speaking at a wedding remember that some of the guests may be standing as they listen to you, that many of them would rather carry on drinking than listen to interminable speeches, and that most of them will have been to weddings before and heard all the 'wedding speech standards' from 'The best way to preserve a wedding ring is to dip it in dish-water three times a day', to 'Always get married in the morning, that way if it doesn't work out you haven't wasted the whole day.'

If there is a toastmaster at the wedding reception, he will announce the speakers. When there is no toastmaster, it is the responsibility of the best man to silence the guests and announce the speakers.

The order of the speakers is as follows:

Father of the Bride

The task of the bride's father (or the man giving her away if the mother is a widow) is to propose a toast to the bride and groom. His speech should be between three and five minutes long.

At the last wedding I attended (not as the father of the bride – my daughters are five and six at the moment!) the bride's father began his speech like this:

'Ladies and gentlemen, friends, today has been a very happy day for us all, and nobody in this room looks happier than the couple sitting here. Doreen looks happy because she's gained David and lost me! I'm happy because he's taken her off my hands! No, seriously, it's always sad to lose a daughter, but my wife and I know that she could not have made a better choice than David.

'They do say that marriages are made in heaven, but don't you believe it. This one was made in our front room last Christmas ...'

He ended with the toast:

' ... and so I ask you to join me in raising your glasses and drink a toast of long life, good health and great happiness to the bride and groom.'

The speech would have been a triumph if everyone had had something in their glasses with which to drink the toast. The lesson here is to double-check that all the glasses have been charged *before* you embark on your speech.

Bridegroom

The bridegroom follows his father-in-law and proposes a toast to the bridesmaids.

At the same wedding, this speech was surprisingly successful:

'Ladies and gentlemen, at the risk of sounding like royalty, my wife and I (and I've been longing to be able to say that!), would like to say a very sincere "thank you" to everyone here for helping to make our special day just that. We would like to thank you all too for your wonderful presents. Surprisingly we haven't acquired half a dozen toasters or ten toast racks, which is lucky really, because we don't eat breakfast.

'For myself, I would like to thank Doreen's parents – if it wasn't for them I wouldn't be standing here today! And I promise that I will never make any mother-in-law jokes. They say that a girl grows to be like her mother, well I only hope it is true in Doreen's case ...'

The groom ended the speech with the toast, and fortunately this time the glasses had been charged.

'Three young ladies today have behaved so well and have done a marvellous job in helping Doreen up the aisle (although I hope she came of her own free will!), and for giving her support I would like to propose a toast, ladies and gentlemen – the bridesmaids.'

The Best Man
The best man replies on behalf of the bridesmaids and having done so reads the greetings telegrams.

This best man began like this:

'Ladies and gentlemen, as has been said already, today is a happy day. Happy for me because I didn't lose the wedding ring, and especially happy for Doreen and David.

'Mr Brown said that this marriage was made in his front room; well I feel I had a little hand in it too, because I was the one who introduced them. Modestly I could say that we wouldn't be here today if it wasn't for me – but I'm not modest! I want no thanks for this, all I ask is that you name your first child after me! Let's hope it isn't a girl because I'd hate her to go through life with a name like Reg. If you *do* have a daughter, I can only hope that she is as lovely as these bridesmaids here today. Don't they look beautiful? David was right to say what a marvellous job they have done. I would like to wish Doreen and David every happiness as they go through life together, and to say thank you most sincerely on behalf of the bridesmaids.'

The best man should be amusing, but never *risqué*. A little flippancy is all very well, but anything remotely offensive or cynical should be avoided at all costs. He should be at least as brief as the father of the bride and the groom, especially if he has telegrams, telemessages and special greetings to read out as well.

Before reading out the messages to the guests, he should have opened them, checked them and sorted them into a rough order, allowing the most 'important' to be read out last. If possible he should first find out who the messages are from, so as to avoid baffling the majority of guests by baldly declaring 'Best of luck – Bess and Ron.' The briefest preamble to each message is all that's required: 'This is a telegram from the bride's aunt and uncle in Australia: "Best of luck – signed Bess and Ron." '

To bring the reading of the telegrams to a neat and effective conclusion, the best man might like to introduce an extra telegram of his own: 'Finally, we seem to have a telegram here from someone calling himself George Bernard Shaw: "Marriage is so popular because it combines the maximum of temptation with the maximum of opportunity." '

Appropriate quotations can either be used as 'celebrity telegrams' or as part of one of the speeches. But beware of cynical statements of any kind. Believe it or not, *all* marriages are happy (it's the living together afterwards that causes the trouble) and to be successful the speeches at a wedding should be suitably sentimental and optimistic.

5

THE RAW MATERIAL

Sources
The sources of material for your speeches are as wide and varied as the speeches themselves.

1. *Magazines*. These provide a wealth of ideas with true-life stories, interviews and practical information. Try not to quote directly, but if you do so, acknowledge your source. It would be wrong to claim an idea as your own if it is not, quite apart from the danger of being tripped up by a member of your audience. Suitable items can be filed away for future reference.

2. *Newspapers*. These also provide much useful factual information and have the advantage of being up to date. If you keep old newspaper cuttings, be sure to date them. Newspapers provide topical material, which will give the impression that you have your finger on the pulse of the nation.
   Be cautious in using anything less than twenty-four hours old as some members of the audience may not have heard it. By all means quote the latest football scores, or some such information, but don't use the joke about the MP and the traffic warden if the news of the local Member of Parliament who struck a meter-maid only appeared in the Stop Press that evening.
   If you are speaking in an area that you have never previously visited, local newspapers can be an invaluable source of background material.

3. *Reference books*. All information you use should be checked in

reference books. An afternoon in the public library can be time well spent in ensuring you have your facts right. Also jot down the source, so that if challenged you can meet it.

4. *Dictionaries of quotations.* Such dictionaries are widely available and are the stock-in-trade of many public speakers. (See bibliography on page 139.) You may have a certain quote in mind: the book will help you to check the wording and confirm the source. Misquoting is most unprofessional, as is crediting the wrong person with the remark. You would look foolish if you confidently claimed a remark to be that of Lord Byron when somebody in your audience knows it was Groucho Marx. So double-check.

Also when quoting take pains to ensure that you do not slander anybody by taking a remark out of context or giving it the wrong connotations.

5. *Television and radio.* These can spark off thoughts that help along an interesting speech. Do not be afraid to say, 'The other evening I saw on television a distressing programme about ... some of you may have seen it. It dealt with the subject in a sympathetic and realistic manner, but it highlighted the fact that ... ' Use what you have seen or heard as a springboard for your own ideas.

6. *Experts.* In any particular field are experts who are often more than happy to help you with a problem of factual affirmation. This is another reason why early planning is an advantage; it gives you time to write to an expert, or an organization, and their reply will be grist to your mill. Always, of course, enclose a stamped, addressed envelope with a request for information, and keep your questions to a minimum.

Never demand information or request that anything confidential be revealed, and do not allow the so-called expert to become unwittingly involved in a matter of great controversy. They should be used only to add weight to your argument and as a source of confirming what you believe to be true.

7. *Other people's material.* On the professional speaking circuit it is supposedly 'not done' to steal other people's jokes and stories, but, of course, it happens all the time. If you do 'borrow' another person's material, avoid reusing it at a function he might be attending or with an audience who might have heard him before. And always change anybody else's stories around to make them completely your own and tell them in your own words.

8. *Personal experiences.* These are the most satisfactory sources for your speech, because then there is no question of credibility, authenticity or originality. Make notes of incidents that amuse you, things you overhear, or that are experienced by you, your family or friends. You can change these experiences around to make it appear they happened to you, so long as you ask permission first – or you might have an experience you don't relish.

How to Adapt the Material
1. If telling a joke or story from a book always tell it in your own words, because the written word is different from the spoken word.

2. Keep all the material modern. If you resort to old joke books you will find stories about 'old maids', pre-decimal coins, trams and so on, which will make your speech seem very old hat.

3. Use only characters and places that people know. If you are in a strange town try to find out something about the area. Pantomimes and club acts always get a big response from their audience when a local village, well-known shop or local hostelry are mentioned. It shows that you have done your homework and personalises the speech.

4. Vary your locations throughout your speech. It would be foolish, for example, to tell several stories about people whom you met in pubs, as your audience will think 'this bloke must spend all his life in pubs'. A restaurant, office, railway carriage and so on, can all be places your audience can identify with.

If you are giving a speech in Geordie-land, it would be pointless to talk about someone you met in a club in London; better to say the name of a well-known location in Newcastle that your listeners will know.

5. Believe in your material and only use items you feel happy with. Say, for example, 'I heard this wonderful story about … ' and *never* 'You've probably heard this before but … ' as that shows a defeatist attitude and almost appears as if you are apologizing for your speech. If you feel apologetic about your material then you should not be using it.

Use of Humour in Speeches

Lord Altrincham, a very witty after-dinner speaker, once remarked that humour in speeches should be 'like the quality of mercy, not strained'.

Humour has two main functions: it adds enjoyment, and it should contribute a point to help further your objective.

Humour should be used to illustrate your main points and, where possible, should be telling as well as entertaining. For example, an hilarious account of chaos within a government department could have the underlying message 'Don't do as we do, do as we say.'

Remember that speaking in public should not be regarded as a vaudeville act – and the public speaker should avoid telling a string of jokes simply 'to get the laughs'. Use humour for a purpose.

Use of Visual Material

Some speeches, especially those with an educational or commercial emphasis, can benefit greatly from the use of visual material and exhibits. Imagine, for example, that somebody had never in their life seen a chair. How would you describe this piece of furniture? What kind of picture will you conjure up if you mention legs, seats, backs, arms? Probably nothing like what a chair looks like. But show a *picture* of a chair – and hey presto, problem solved.

This can apply to speeches. Something may be too

complicated to demonstrate verbally, and if this is the case by all means use a visual aid. Keep it simple: video tapes, films, sound recordings, slides, charts etc. can be invaluable accessories, so long as using them doesn't hold up the proceedings and effectively obscures rather than illuminates the matter in hand. With all the magnificent technology of the electronic audio-visual age, there is sometimes a tendency for the medium to swamp the message.

That said, don't be frightened of visual aids. You can *tell* of a house infested with rats, *tell* them there were hundreds, but *show* them a picture of the chaos and devastation, and it will say more than a thousand words. Psychologists tell us that our conceptions and outlooks are influenced 85 per cent through what we see; 9 per cent through what we hear; and 6 per cent through our other senses.

Of course a well-chosen visual aid when making an appeal of any kind can help arouse sympathy, and you will find, especially when dealing with young people, that an audience's interest will be held much longer if it can see something other than just you, the speaker.

If relevant, a simple chart can be used for reference throughout your speech and enable you to summarize specific points. If your speech or lecture does happen to be about a complicated topic, the use of visual material will make it easier to follow. Not only will a visual aid make you look more professional, it will help you keep on the right track too and not wander from the point.

Dangers of Visual Material
Use of visuals can have its pitfalls. Here are the main dangers to avoid:

1. *Exhibits or charts that are too small.* Whatever your visual medium, it must be large enough and clear enough for everyone to see. If you have brought in a rare eighth-century manuscript, one or two people in the front row might be able to see it, but the other 250 people in the hall will feel you have wasted your time.

2. *Charts that are too complicated.* Nothing should be cluttered

or too subtle. If a chart cannot be easily understood by all, it should not be used.

3. *Inadequate explanation of a visual aid.* If you are using a chart or slide, do explain it fully. Don't just say, 'In this print of Hogarth's *The Rake's Progress* you will see ...' Say instead: 'If you look carefully in the bottom right-hand corner of the picture ...' This makes it more explicit.

4. *Irrelevant visual material.* Just because you happen to have a picture of soldiers in the trenches in the First World War and it is vaguely connected with your speech on Dylan Thomas, it does not mean that you are bound to use it. Never use a visual just for the sake of it.

5. *Badly rehearsed use of visuals.* Slides can be an absolute disaster if their sequence is not properly rehearsed. We've all seen comedy sketches where the slide operator drops the box and muddles all the slides up, so that when the speaker says: 'And here we see the winner at Crufts for the Best Bitch of the Year' there appears a picture of the mayoress on the screen. These things happen in reality too. Number all slides carefully and rehearse fully so that anyone helping you is familiar with the cues.

6. *Supposedly 'hidden' exhibits.* Nothing is worse than a speaker who has something covered with a sheet standing beside him that he intends to reveal later. He speaks as if it is invisible whilst the audience contemplates what the object is, oblivious to what the speaker is saying. Either keep your exhibit completely out of sight until required or stand it openly in full view of the audience but where it will not distract from you.

7. *Technical hitches.* If you are using any electronic audio-visual equipment, make sure the screen and speakers are properly adjusted *before* you start and have someone operating the equipment who knows what they are doing.

8. *Disasters*. Be prepared for the worst. The day will come when you forget the tape or the slides or the charts: be ready to cope without them if you have to.

Use of Vocabulary

A vast vocabulary and knowledge of long words is not a necessary qualification for a speaker, but the *choice* of words is important.

Just think of two of the most memorable of all speeches, one fiction, one non-fiction:

Sydney Carton's 'It is a far, far better thing that I do than I have ever done. It is a far, far better rest that I go to than I have ever known.'

Winston Churchill's 'We shall defend our island, whatever the cost may be; we shall fight on the beaches, we shall fight on the landing grounds, we shall fight in the fields and in the streets, we shall fight in the hills; we shall never surrender.'

Such simple vocabulary, but how effectively it was put to use! When writing your speeches use words and phrases that come most naturally to you, but check that you do not use one particular word too many times. For example, if you find you have used the word 'important' fifteen times, look in a thesaurus of English words and you will find a host of alternatives that will give variety and colour to your speech.

Make a list of words that you find strong and powerful and use them in your speech. Make up original similes. Better perhaps to say, 'He got out as though he'd just seen a tax inspector ... ' than 'He ran out like a cat on a hot tin roof.'

Check your speech to make certain that it is grammatically correct, and cut out any unnecessary words. All too often you can hear speakers say 'At this point in time ... ' when all they mean is 'Now'.

Pay special and particular attention to pronunciation and the definitions of words. Most dictionaries demonstrate correct pronunciation as well as providing definitions, so that if you feel uncertain about any of the words you plan to use, check them out first. And do make quite certain that your speech is not punctuated with 'ers' or sprinkled liberally with 'you knows', 'you sees' or 'sort ofs'. These really can be very irritating to your listeners and are simply avoided by knowing what you are going to say and saying it calmly and confidently.

For a simple set of rules for effective 'good' English, it would be difficult to better the six offered by George Orwell in 1946:

1. Never use a metaphor, simile, or other figure of speech which you are used to seeing in print.
2. Never use a long word where a short one will do.
3. If it is possible to cut a word, always cut it out.
4. Never use the passive where you can use the active.
5. Never use a foreign phrase, a scientific word, or a jargon word if you can think of an everyday English equivalent.
6. Break any of these rules sooner than say anything outright barbarous.

Orwell, of course, was referring to written English, but if you follow his rules as a speaker your language will be clear, uncluttered, pungent and to the point. What's more, as Orwell noted, 'When you make a stupid remark its stupidity will be obvious, even to yourself.'

Speech Devices

The following devices can be used to introduce material into your speech, none of them need necessarily be humorous.

1. *Anecdotes*. A personal anecdote is one of the best methods of introducing any subject into your speech. Such a personal story can be on any subject from misunderstandings with your garage mechanic, to a defective dishwasher which always answers back. In fact, any kind of situation in which you have found yourself and which the listener can identify with. Whatever the subject of your speech, you should be able to think of a personal experience, and the lesson you learned from it, if any.

2. *Conversations*. Overheard conversations, or snatches of them, are a marvellous way of using material. Such 'eavesdroppings' can add life and colour to your speech.

'Two women were behind me at the post office and one was

recounting how her car broke down in Ireland. "Well, why didn't you go and stay in a hotel," asked her friend.

' "Oh no, we couldn't do that, you see the nearest hotel was five miles in one direction and twelve miles in the other direction." '

If you hear an amusing joke that has a good punchline which is right for your speech, then change it to something you overheard. But if you hear a professional comic's joke and you want desperately to use it, be sure to credit him with it. For example you may have heard Les Dawson on television use this routine:

'I've always tried to be a success in life, not just to please my wife, but to spite my mother-in-law. Having been successful I have at last managed to afford a brand new car, but the other day I felt very mixed emotions – the wife's mother drove it over a cliff.'

In your speech you may have got to a point where a definition of 'mixed emotion' would be relevant, so say 'Last week on TV I heard Les Dawson define mixed emotions ... ' etc. The audience will prick up their ears because they want to hear what Les Dawson said, and because, by identifying yourself with a popular personality, you have made yourself seem human and shown that you have the same tastes as the audience. Also, others will listen to hear what they missed on television.

It is infinitely preferable to claiming a characteristically Les Dawson story as your own.

3. *Characters.*
   a) Use people that the listeners know: 'I used to go to college with your chairman, Horace Freeman ...' or, 'I married your president's daughter, and not many of you will know this about him, but ...'

      By using people and characters that the audience know you are certain to gain their attention. Do not, however, say anything detrimental or cause embarrassment to the person you are talking about.
   b) Use your own family. People seem to love to hear domestic stories about husband-and-wife repartee, and you can bring your family into the situation:

      'As I was coming here this evening, my husband asked

me what I intended to talk about. I told him Ancient
Greece, and asked him if he knew where the Acropolis
was. "How do I know?" he replied, "You should
remember where you put things." '

c)   Use your neighbours and friends. Always identify them by
name, i.e. 'My neighbour, Mrs Green … ', as it enables the
hearer to have a mental picture of that person.

d)   Use professional people, such as doctors, policemen or
lawyers, that your listeners may have had dealings with
and again can identify with.

4. *Possessions*. Your belongings can provide a useful way of
making a particular point – a small item of sentimental value
say, or the one thing you wanted to have all your life and what a
disappointment it was when you finally got it – in fact anything
from your car, your clothes, your pets, your house … the list is
endless. Tell the story about the possession, and show the
relevance of the experience to the subject of your speech.

5. *News items*. A news item can be something you heard on
television which adds weight to your argument, or a newspaper
article.

On a lighter note it can be made up news about the new
banana diet that won't make you slim but you'll be fantastic at
climbing trees, or the new nightclub where the meals are so
expensive that one look at the menu and you lose your appetite.

6. *Poetry and quotations*. You can lead into your subject with an
apposite poem:

Here lies a chump who got no gain
From jumping on a moving train.
Banana skins on platform seven
Ensured his terminus was Heaven.

'That may seem an amusing epitaph, but passenger safety on the
railways is an increasing problem, made worse by the
carelessness of the passengers themselves …'

Or an apt quotation:

'Of a violinist's playing, Doctor Samuel Johnson is reputed to have said: "Difficult do you call it, sir? I wish it were impossible." '

A regular public speaker will build up his or her own library of dictionaries of quotations, but should resist the temptation to use more than one quotation per speech. The listeners, after all, have come to hear what *you* have got to say.

6

SPEAKING IN COMMITTEE

Having served on a number of committees in my time, I have no hesitation in endorsing the view that a committee is: 'A group of people who individually can do nothing, but collectively can meet and decide that nothing can be done.'

Whatever you may feel about committees, if you belong to one and want to make your presence felt in it, you must learn to master the very special, and rather different, craft of 'speaking in committee'. Unlike the platform speaker, the committee member should in no way set out to impress; the aim is to *convince* not show off. If you are convincing enough then committee members will be impressed by your ideas anyway.

The vital point to bear in mind, and this cannot be emphasized enough, it that preparation is of paramount importance if you are to succeed in committee life. If you have proposals to put forward, amendments to make to company policy or changes to the constitution, you must have facts to support your suggestions. Do not be afraid to use charts and graphs, and have photocopies ready so that you can present each committee member with a copy.

The organized and well-equipped committee member should have little trouble convincing his fellow members that his proposals are sound. Remember that people love to *buy* but hate to be *sold* and the good committee member will bring others round to his way of thinking with concrete evidence, rather than demanding that his ideas *must* be adopted.

Be simple in your presentation and vocabulary, especially

when making reports. Clear description of events is preferable to bombarding everyone with verbiage and jargon.

One of the most difficult and demanding positions on any committee is that of the chairman.

The Art of Chairing a Committee

The chairman (or chairwoman or chairperson) should be in complete control of the meeting and never allow the proceedings to get out of hand or behind schedule. The success of any committee will be determined by the chairman, and it is a job that requires tact, sensitivity, patience, and at times, a keen sense of humour.

The chairman has several important functions:

a) He sets the tone of the whole meeting. He should prepare the agenda well in advance and make sure that it is adhered to.

b) He is in control of the time and in his opening remarks should advise that everyone keep within his or her allotted time (for example, five minutes each).

c) If the committee gets sidetracked it is the chairman's duty to bring the meeting back to a discussion of the main points.

d) A good chairman will encourage co-operation at meetings and establish team-work.

e) He should prevent anyone from monopolizing the meeting, and tactfully stop someone from going on too long.

f) The chairman should summarize the meeting and delegate duties.

Perhaps the most important quality for a chairman is tact. He needs to encourage speakers who do not express themselves very well. If someone has difficulty in putting across his ideas, the good chairman will compliment the speaker and then repeat the points in a clearer and more understandable manner.

But he will not do this by saying, 'What John really means is ...' or 'What John is trying to say ...'

Rather he will say, 'Thank you John, for that very constructive suggestion. So as John rightly points out ...'

In this way John will feel valued and is more likely to give full co-operation.

The chairman should also prevent the overheated arguments

that frequently occur in committee rooms. These should be nipped in the bud before the fur starts flying.

Annual General Meetings

These follow a general pattern and an agenda should be formulated and adhered to. This is a typical agenda:

Agenda

1. Chairman's welcome.
2. Apologies for absence.
3. Minutes of last AGM.
4. Matters arising from these minutes.
5. Annual reports.
6. Any other business.
7. Date and time of next meeting.

Following a few words of welcome, the chairman should then call upon the secretary to read the minutes of the previous annual general meeting. It is up to the chairman to follow the agenda and call upon the people present to perform these duties. Frequently the secretary makes no further speech but continues taking the minutes of the current meeting, and the chairman should find out whether or not particular reports are to be made beforehand.

After the reading of the minutes the chairman should ask if there are any matters arising from these. Usually some developments will have taken place within the last year and will need commenting upon.

The discussion that follows should not be allowed to continue too long, and then come the annual reports. These should be kept brief and can be read. This is one occasion when a speech can be read. The advantage of this is accuracy, continuity and brevity.

Chairman's Report

Here is an example of how the chairman's report should be written. Choose the main points that you have to mention, and say a little about each.

Chairman of Blanktown Parish Council
Report for 198- to 198-

1. *Maintenance of Roads.*

During the year the long-overdue repairs have been carried out to the roadsides between Hill View and Trubshore Road corner. The cost was £x, slightly lower than we anticipated.

2. *The former primary school: Blanford Prior.*

There is still no news of any development with regard to the use of the old school buildings and schoolhouse. The Parish Council has asked to be kept informed if and when anything is considered for this building. The caravans that have been an eyesore in the school yard for so long have at last been removed. The playing field fence has been re-erected and repaired where necessary by Brick Builders Ltd, and at no cost to the Parish Council.

3. *Litter.*

A successful 'litter picking' day was held in the spring, and it is hoped that a similar event will take place next year.

4. *Clerk to the Parish Council.*

At the Parish Council meeting of 12th August, the Council confirmed the appointment of Mr Rupert Smith as clerk to the Parish Council. The Council's thanks and best wishes go with the retiring clerk, Mrs Susan Jones, who has left the district.

Having concluded his speech the chairman should then call upon the next member of the committee to give his or her report. Assuming that having read the minutes, the secretary has no other report, the next speech is likely to come from the treasurer.

Treasurer's Report

In order to enable the auditor to have more time to look at the accounts before the AGM, it was decided last year to take the financial year to the end of September instead of the end of October. Thus the financial year of 198-/8- has been only 11 months.

You can see from the balance at the End of Year (Item 16) that we end the year in a similar position to last year with a small surplus.

Cost increases continue relentlessly. For example the surplus for the first six months was £920.85, whereas for the second half it was only £354.21, despite our efforts to reduce expenditure. In response to the plea from the Borough Council to keep our expenditure as low as possible during the coming year, in view of the current economic recession, the Parish Council asked for the same Precept (money that we ask for from the Borough Council) this year as last year, £4,500.

All in all, I am relieved to be able to report that we have had a very stable financial year.

Other Reports

Each member of the committee, or those holding an official position, may be called upon to give a report. No report need be very long and five minutes should be the absolute limit. It should be entirely factual, giving an account of particular events and situations. Nothing more.

Question Time

Occasionally at committee meetings, and especially annual general meetings, the chairman allows questions to be asked of the committee members. This should be orderly and controlled, and is the responsibility of the chairman alone. It should be made clear that questions must not be shouted out, and that those wishing to ask a question should just raise their hand.

The chairman should give each person a fair chance to ask a question and not allow one person to monopolize the proceedings or turn it into a general discussion. The chairman should repeat the question asked – this makes it clear to everyone in the room exactly what has been asked, and gives the person to whom it has been addressed sufficient time to compose a short answer.

Questions must be asked one at a time and the chairman must clarify anything that is not immediately clear. Members of the public always appreciate an opportunity to ask questions at first hand about points they feel should have greater attention.

Anyone answering questions should do so concisely, taking care not to become involved in any arguments or heated discussions.

Closing a Committee Meeting

Bringing a committee meeting to a close is once again the task of the chairman. He should make certain that the meeting does not overrun its time limit and tactfully bring the meeting to an end.

'Ladies and gentlemen, unfortunately it is getting late and we are running out of time. I would like to thank everyone who has attended the meeting for their valuable contributions and I am sure you will feel that we have made some headway. Will you please note the date of the next committee meeting, Monday 23rd April, and I shall look forward to seeing you then, at 3.25 p.m. I now officially declare the meeting closed.'

Secrets of Success

The successful committee member will know what he or she wants to get out of a committee and will set about getting it in a firm but friendly way. Tub-thumping oratory is out of place in committee. A more subtle, sensitive approach is needed: 'Softly, softly catchee money' is the motto here.

If you have a proposal to make that you suspect will prove controversial and will almost certainly be opposed, state your case as simply and as calmly as you can. Let the opposition get heated if they must, but at all times 'keep your cool'. Be sure to let your opponents have their say: don't interrupt them or try to correct them while they are speaking. Let them exhaust themselves before you return to the fray and reiterate your points with clarity and emphasis, but without unnecessary huffing and puffing and with all the good humour you can muster.

Of course, if you have the chairman on your side it helps enormously because you can stage-manage the timing of your proposal. If the committee meeting starts at 6.00 p.m. and is scheduled to finish by 7.00 p.m. you don't want your item to be placed too high up on the agenda or you will find that the discussion of it becomes prolonged and the opposition may have time to marshall their arguments and muster support against you. However, put your proposal towards the end of the meeting, and, providing enough time is available for a reasonable if limited discussion, you should be able to win the argument before it gets out of hand, simply by virtue of the fact that the uncommitted members of the committee have their eyes on the clock and will be happy to bring the issue to a vote and side with the apparently more reasonable side!

A successful committee chairman should do his best to be and *be seen to be* fair to all the members of the committee. This can mean actually giving more time to 'unreasonable' members than to 'reasonable' ones, in order to let the 'unreasonable' ones feel that they have had their say and so shut them up. Obviously the chairman should not allow any one member to dominate or bully the rest of the committee and he should never allow the chair's authority to be weakened by letting a discussion get out of hand. If tempers are getting raised and two sides in an argument are becoming increasingly intemperate, an effective ploy is to turn to a third party – especially one who is noted for his calm, dispassionate approach to all things controversial – and invite that party to make a contribution to the discussion at this stage.

If the worst comes to the worst and the discussion seems to be in danger of degenerating into a brawl, the wise chairman will bring the issue to a close by proposing that further discussion of the issue be postponed to a later meeting. This will provide a 'cooling off' period and enable the chairman to arrange that, at the next meeting, all sides are represented and know that they have x minutes in which to put their respective cases and no more, after which a vote will be taken and that will be that. There are times when a chairman may be forced to assume the mantle of the benevolent dictator, but as a rule he should model himself on a benevolent elder statesman, above party, above suspicion, but never above himself.

7

DEBATING

The aim of argument, or of discussion, should not be victory,
but progress.   Joseph Joubert

For the inexperienced or nervous speaker, one of the best ways of
learning the art of public speaking and conquering fear is to take
part in a debate. Debating encourages quick thinking and gives
valuable practice in putting thoughts into words in front of an
audience.

Anyone who has had experience of debates will find the
progression into local councils and government a natural process,
because debating makes one particularly adept at putting
forward a convincing argument.

Purpose of Debate

a)   To give people an opportunity openly to express their
views and ideas.

b)   To acquire knowledge and insight into a particular
subject.

c)   To reach a reasonable and satisfactory conclusion.

Winning a debate or argument is not the most important issue,
although it is gratifying if the majority agree with you. The
object is to enjoy the chance of making your views publicly
known. It teaches you self-discipline whilst speaking and at the
same time it is hoped you will learn something yourself. If
speakers both for and against the motion have done their
homework thoroughly, your knowledge of the subject under

discussion is bound to improve.

Techniques of Debate

1. Once you know the motion to be debated make a list of all the advantages and disadvantages on two sheets of paper, before deciding whether you are 'for' or 'against'. By looking at the subject from all sides you will be able to fire back at your opponents.

2. Decide which side of the fence you fall on – taking into consideration what you think the reactions of the audience will be. If you are a complete beginner, speak for the side in which you believe. That way you will be much more convincing.

3. Begin compiling your ammunition, using newspapers, encyclopaedias, reference books, etc. The more facts you have to back up your argument the better, and the more confident you yourself will be. One problem the beginner often encounters is that there are *too many* facts and so much to say on the subject that he doesn't know where to start. Don't make the mistake of thinking you have to use *all* the facts. Take only the major points and leave the remaining ones for other speakers to comment on. To attempt to pack every argument into your speech will only result in mental indigestion among your audience. Always have more goods in the shop than you display in the window.

4. Check and double-check your information to avoid making a fool of yourself. Think of Sophocles – 'It is terrible to speak well and be wrong.' Write down all your information first without making any attempt to order it.

5. Having compiled your list, one of the simplest methods of putting the material into order is to take a pair of scissors and cut your notes into strips. You can then order the strips into the best combination of facts, putting those that you feel should go together next to each other.

6. Once your facts are ordered the bulk of your speech is

prepared. Go through adding any extra evidence to support your argument. Think of links to join your points together. There must be some overall unity to your speech.

7. Now you can make simple notes with headings on a postcard to remind you of each point as you speak. The use of different coloured inks can be helpful – red for headings, blue for specific points, and so on.

8. Become enthusiastic about your subject and let yourself go when you speak. Nothing great was ever achieved without enthusiasm. As Clarence Day put it: 'You can't sweep other people off their feet if you can't be swept off your own.'

Speaking Techniques to Remember
1. Keep your speech informal and brief, using a conversational tone. If you talk *to* your audience, rather than *at* them, you will make a more favourable impression and be more fluent. Keep your sentences short. Avoid fancy words, and use 'you' and 'yours' to include the listeners.

2. Speak clearly and confidently at moderate speed; if you speak too quickly you will lose your listeners, and if too slowly you will lose the momentum of your speech.

3. Don't try to be too clever. The speaker who attempts to be over-subtle, sarcastic, or bigheaded will not go down well with any audience. Be sincere.

4. Don't use jokes or anecdotes. You can be amusing and witty if you wish, but do not make a deliberate attempt to be funny. If it comes naturally the audience will appreciate it, but forced humour for its own sake is irritating in the context of a serious debate.

5. Don't embarrass or slander your opponent. That will only lead to trouble. Not only is it discourteous it is also bad policy and will gain you nothing. By all means disagree with your

opposition but do not turn the occasion into a public slanging match. If you throw mud, you may miss your mark but your hands will still be dirty.

6. Avoid anything that will put a barrier between you and your audience. Do not say anything that is going to distance them by leaving them in doubt about your true feelings.

7. Don't repeat yourself, and if you forget to say something, leave it out altogether rather than go back over the same ground. If the point is essential to your argument then come back to it by introducing it as a new topic.

8. Treat the art of debating like a game – a game which, knowing the rules, you try to play fairly using the skills you have acquired and not attempting anything underhand. The voting at the end of any debate is the least important part of the proceedings. Some you win, some you lose.

The Shape of the Debate

The first person to speak in a debate is the Proposer. He is followed by the Opposer. Next comes the speaker seconding the Proposition, followed by the speaker seconding the Opposition. At this stage the debate is usually thrown open to the floor and the chairman invites brief contributions from the audience, taking those who wish to speak for and against in strict rotation.

After the floor debate, the original Proposer and Opposer will be invited to sum up, before the vote is taken.

Any speech made in a debate requires tight control and careful structuring.

1. Begin with a general introduction to the subject. Make it watertight with hard facts, stating exactly what your views are.

2. Say exactly how the subject affects members of the audience themselves. This makes it more relevant.

3. Reply to any points raised by your opponents which have not

already been effectively dealt with by other speakers on your side.

4. Save your best point until last to make the greatest impact, leaving no doubts as to where you stand. The final punch will make all the difference.

How to Form Your Own Debating Society

If you would like to join a debating society, and can't find one to join, form your own instead.

The simplest way to begin is with a group of friends. If you do not have any friends who are sufficiently enthusiastic, an advertisement in your local newspaper is an excellent way of letting local people know of your plan and of gaining support.

Having mustered the people together, form a committee which can draw up a constitution to deal with all matters appertaining to the Society. The members should be:

The Chairman or President

This can be yourself as organizer, or someone whom members feel would be a good chairman at meetings, preside over the debates, and see that the rules are adhered to. He or she must see that proper conduct is maintained and disorder ruled out. In the chairman's absence, a vice-chairman can be appointed to take over the duties, but this is not an essential position on the committee unless it happens to be a very large organization.

Chairing a debate is easier than chairing a committee because the rules of debate are clear-cut and all the chairman has to do is enforce them. Before the debate begins advise all the main speakers as to the allowed length of their speeches. If the Proposer and Opposer are to be allowed ten minutes each, make it clear to them that ten minutes is their absolute limit.

Speakers who take longer than they should can bedevil a debate and one effective way of dealing with them is to equip the secretary with two cards: one marked 'TWO MINUTES MORE', the other 'TIME UP'. After a speaker has been on his feet for eight minutes the secretary should discreetly pass him the first card and two minutes later the second. If a minute or more after this the speaker is clearly no nearer his conclusion, the chairman should intervene and say, 'I must ask the speaker to finish his speech now' and then allow him no more than thirty seconds in which to wrap up his argument and sit down.

Before speeches are invited from the floor the chairman should make it clear how long they may last. If, say, four minutes is the limit, the chairman should tolerate five, but then intervene and ask the speaker to promptly bring his argument to a close.

Some debating societies allow members to interrupt the debate at any stage with 'points of order' or 'points of information'. If a member raises a point of order, the person who is speaking must give way and sit down while the point of order is dealt with by the chairman. Points of order can only relate to the rules and procedures of debate and their possible infringement. Once a point of order has been raised the chairman should deal with it immediately and then let the debate proceed.

A member can raise a point of information only if he has a question to ask or a relevant point to make that arises directly out of what the speaker is saying. The member wishing to raise a point of information should simply get to his feet and announce 'Point of information.' The chairman should then ask the speaker whether or not he is prepared to take the point of information. The speaker is in no way obliged to do so. If the speaker agrees to take the point of information he will sit down while the member makes the point, which he should do as succinctly as possible. The speaker should then rise to his feet, answer the point and carry on. If the speaker does not wish to concede the point, he may carry on speaking without interruption and the member wanting to raise the point should sit down again immediately. The chairman should see to it that points of information are only raised by members genuinely seeking information: all too often points of information are raised by members eager to score debating points from the floor and anxious to interrupt the main speaker's flow with a mini-speech of their own. It is up to the chairman to see this doesn't happen.

Secretary
The secretary is a vital member of any society. He or she should deal with all correspondence, take the minutes of meetings, give

notices and announcements, and deal with the general administration. In a small society the secretary will also deal with financial matters. It need not necessarily be someone interested in actual debating, but rather someone with administrative skills, who enjoys such duties.

Treasurer

A treasurer is necessary if the membership is very large. Amongst you there is sure to be someone who is at home with figures. The committee as a whole should decide upon a suitable subscription fee and it is the treasurer's task to make sure that each member is fully paid up. He will be responsible for opening a bank account in the society's name, dealing with the annual accounts, and making sure there is a small surplus at the end of the year. He or she will also be responsible for any outgoings on behalf of the society.

Committee Members

There can be as many or as few other members as you wish. Preferably no less than three, besides the above mentioned, and not more than seven. Some of these should have a special interest in debating so as to deal constructively with matters pertaining to the debates themselves. Others should be useful from a purely social point of view, such as fund-raising, social functions, and general helping.

Other special officers can be appointed, such as a publicity officer, membership secretary, promotions officer (responsible for inviting guest speakers). But this is a matter of choice, and no other named positions other than chairman, secretary and treasurer are really necessary.

Having formed the committee, their first task should be to decide upon a name for the society and to draw up a set of rules. These rules can be amended from time to time, but are essential to have so as to avoid chaos. Take care also when choosing a name that it is not going to put people off joining (i.e. The Blanktown Chinwag Society). Check too that if your society is abbreviated to just its initial letters, the result does not spell an inappropriate word.

The Rules

The rules must be drawn up by the committee and should be given to every member on payment of his membership fee. By ensuring that every member has a copy you can then enforce the rules.

Here is a specimen set of rules that can be adapted to suit your own society.

1.   The society shall be known as The Blankford Debating Society.

2.   The society shall meet each Tuesday evening at 7.30 p.m. in the Church Hall unless otherwise determined by the committee.

3.   The committee shall consist of a chairman, secretary and treasurer, together with five members of the society. All members of the committee shall retire at the annual general meeting and shall be eligible for re-election.

4.   In the absence of the chairman at any meeting, another member of the committee shall take his place, as agreed by the members present.

5.   Speakers at debates shall be allowed up to fifteen minutes each maximum. Openers of debates fifteen minutes; subsequent speakers ten minutes or less, at the discretion of the chairman. All speeches shall be open to criticism and discussion.

6.   Members shall be at liberty to introduce their friends to all ordinary meetings of the society. Visitors may take part in the discussions at the discretion of the chairman.

7.   Written notice of any motion affecting the business of the society shall be given to the secretary and read at the previous meeting to the one at which it is to be proposed.

8.   The chairman shall put to the vote of the meeting all motions duly moved and seconded.

9.   Members only shall be allowed to vote.

10.   Any vacancies that arise in the committee during the course of the year shall be filled at an ordinary meeting of the society.

11.   The annual subscription shall be £5.00, payable on or before 31st March in each year.

12.   No alteration or amendments to these rules can be made except at the annual general meeting of the society, or at an extraordinary general meeting especially called for that purpose by not less than ten members.

Subjects for Debate

Choose subjects about which a great deal can be said both 'for' and 'against'. It would be pointless to propose a motion that a very high percentage of people will be in favour of, because the outcome will be obvious from the outset and it gives little realistic cause for debate. All speakers would prefer a controversial issue that they can get their teeth into.

The number of potential debating topics is infinite, but these are some areas that tend to be popular:

General
Television has caused the death of conversation.
There is life after death.
State support of live theatre should be withdrawn.
Earth is visited by creatures from another planet.
The death penalty should be restored.
There should be free public transport for all.

Political
It would be better to be 'dead than Red'.
British troops should be withdrawn from Northern Ireland.

The United Kingdom should become a nuclear-free zone.
Party government should be abolished.
Our democracy is not truly democratic.
The EEC has failed – Britain should pull out.

Religious

Christianity is out of date.
Homosexual marriages should be allowed.
Divorcees should be allowed to remarry in the Catholic church.
Women should be allowed to become clergymen.
Religious instruction should not be part of the state school
    curriculum.
There is no God.

Economic

The silicon chip is more a menace than a benefit.
Strikers should not receive strike pay.
The abolition of trade unions would result in greater
    productivity.
A boycott of all foreign products would benefit our economy.
The West should double its aid to the Third World overnight.
Money is the root of all evil,

Educational

Private schools should be abolished.
The school leaving age should be raised to eighteen.
Standards in British schools have declined dramatically and are
    still declining.
Students should be expected to pay for their own further
    education.
Teachers should have no more than four weeks' holiday a year.
School exams have no place in an egalitarian society.

Sociological

Old age pensioners should have free heating in their homes.
People with a background of psychiatric instability should be
    considered unfit for parenthood.
Smoking in all public places should be banned.

Persistent rapists should be castrated.
Water should be metered, like gas and electricity.
Cannabis should be legalized.

Ethical
Corporal punishment should be made illegal.
Pornography is a national evil.
Racial prejudice is on the increase.
Euthenasia should be made legal.
Marriage should be made more difficult and divorce easier.
Abortion is murder.

Once you have chosen the theme for the debate a formal
proposal will be formulated. For example, if the debate is to be
about the opening of a sex-shop in the town, the motion might
read: 'This House believes the opening of a sex-shop in
Chelmsford will do damage and should not be permitted.'

Whatever the theme, be it sublime ('This House believes in
the existence of God') or ridiculous ('This House believes that a
drink before and a cigarette after are the three best things in
life'), it is important to remember that debate is about the art of
persuasion. The skilled debater will not be trying to get his
opponents to change their minds – probably a hopeless task – but
he will be doing his best to persuade his audience to come round
to his way of thinking. At the end of every debate a vote is taken
and whichever side of the argument secures most votes has
carried the motion and won the day.

Some debating societies have two votes in the course of the
debate: one at the start and one at the finish. This is an
illuminating exercise because it reveals how many people have
been persuaded to change their attitudes by what they have
heard during the debate. It is also worth while because it
involves the audience both at the beginning and at the end of the
proceedings and will make the members of the audience,
whatever they may be – other members of the debating society,
friends and relatives of the speakers, members of the general
public – feel that they are more than mere spectators: they are
involved and their involvement counts for something.

8

SPEAKING ON TELEVISION AND RADIO

As a public speaker the widest audience you will ever encounter will be if you appear on television or radio. Daily, hundreds of people are interviewed on chat shows, news programmes and in documentaries, and with the advent of breakfast television the opportunities for speakers of all sorts to air their views have become even greater.

It may be as an expert in a particular field that you are called upon to speak; you may be involved in a controversial issue which will put you in demand; you may have an important cause you want to champion. Whatever the reason, you are certain to find that broadcasting is a totally different form of public speaking from any that we have looked at so far. A whole new set of techniques will need to be learnt, and since it may well be that you appear on radio or television only once it has to be right first time.

Television
If you are to appear on television for the first time, it can be a worrying prospect. Interviewers can be ruthless, and quick-thinking on your part is essential – one mistake and you could be the laughing stock of the nation! Preparation and concentration is essential.

Remember that what viewers *see* is as important as what they hear. Consider this when you choose your clothes for the occasion. What kind of image do you wish to project? Looking relaxed is difficult but necessary. Sit still and do not fidget, because every move you make will be magnified.

How do you get on television in the first place? You may be invited to appear because you've won the pools or had quins or been elected as local member of parliament – but if not it *is* possible for an ordinary member of the public to approach television companies should they feel they have an issue to discuss that will be of interest to viewers.

The best way to approach the companies is with a brief letter addressed to the producer of the programme in which you hope to appear, explaining the scheme you are involved in and why it would benefit the viewers to know about it. It may be concerned with a health hazard to children in your town which you want to put a stop to, or you may be attempting to raise money for charity by walking from Land's End to John O'Groats and want to gain support. Whatever it is, if you want to get it on the air, present your idea in a way that makes it appear either important or unusual. Significance, originality and topicality are what television producers are looking for, especially when it comes to 'local items'.

If you just want to appear on TV as an ego trip so that Auntie Marge in Gravesend can see her niece on the telly, then forget it; nobody will appreciate your wasting their time.

If the local television station is intrigued by your letter, they will contact you. If they are not, don't badger them – approach your local newspaper and see if they will interview you instead.

Having shown interest, you may be invited along by the company to discuss the issue first. Eventually a date and time will be set for you to appear.

Television Interviews

The television interview is the most usual method of communication on television. (Unless you are giving a Party Political Broadcast it is highly improbable that you will be given the airwaves to yourself.) Before you undertake the interview there are some points for you to consider.

a.   What type of programme will the interview be used in?
b.   Is it going to be live or recorded?

c. What is the reason for the interview?
d. Will other people be there to debate with you, or put their view to?
e. Will the interview be edited?
f. Who will the interviewer be?
g. What line of questioning will he or she take?
h. When will it be transmitted? (Make sure it is not months later when it could be too late to do you any good.)

Remember that if you are interviewed it is unlikely to be for more than a very few minutes, so you have to pack as much as you possible can into that time. Do not make needless repetitions and give short, simple answers. If an interviewer says: 'Have you discussed this with the Minister of Health?' don't reply, 'Yes, I have discussed this with the Minister of Health.' Valuable seconds have ticked by. Say simply 'Yes.'

Before you are interviewed decide what you hope to get out of it and who you hope to appeal to the most. Think of three main points that you want to put over, and how you can say them as simply and as effectively as you can e.g.:

* Amount of money needed.
* Where it will come from.
* What it will go on.

'For this scheme to work we need £40,000.'

'If each viewer sponsored us for 50p we could reach our target in a week.'

'As a result 1,000 babies' lives would be saved each year.'

These are the kinds of simple statements that you need to make. Be confident and forthright. Never say 'Well, er ... ' before you speak but make bold and positive statements.

'Yes. Exactly. Without it they would die.'

If you come across as a positive personality you are more likely to get positive results.

In the Studio

Once you have made it to the studio you should not be idle and sit and wait until you are on the air. You have much more important things to do.

First, as you are shown into the presenter's rest-room there are nearly always copies of the script lying around. If there aren't then ask to see one. This will tell you the order in which you are appearing and with whom, and what approach the interviewer is going to take. The manner in which he plans to introduce you will give you a clue:

'Over the past ten months research into the rate of infant mortality has given cause for concern. Following the death of her own child, Mrs Sandra Smith has demanded further investigations into the causes, and hopes to raise £40,000 for research. She has joined me today in the studio ...'

If you are appearing because of your own cause, all should be well and you will be given an opportunity to express your opinions, but if you happen to be involved in a more controversial issue – perhaps you are a shop steward who has brought men out on strike over a matter of principle – you will need to check the script to see who else is being interviewed and whether or not a biased angle is to be taken. You will then have time to prepare yourself for attack if necessary.

Ask the person interviewing you what line he intends to take. This is important to know from both sides so that you are both on the same track and the interviewer knows you will not dry up. Be prepared, however, for trick questions. An actress I know was to be interviewed on a popular chat show and made a point of asking the presenter beforehand not to make any reference to her first marriage as she found it embarrassing.

The interview began and the opening question was: 'Ten years ago your marriage to __ __ ended in a blaze of publicity ... ' and proceeded to ask her exactly what she had requested him not to.

Another actor, knowing the interviewer's tactics, implored that no questions be asked about his latest film, as it was all top secret. Naturally the interviewer *did* ask and the wily actor got the publicity he hoped for.

Obviously you will know beforehand which programme you will be appearing on, so watch it first and get to know the type of questions the interviewers usually ask.

Try to relax before you take your position in the studio. Ask to see the set first, where you will have to walk and where you will actually sit, so that you are able to get your bearings. Drink a cup of tea or coffee if you wish, but nothing alcoholic. Half a pint of lager might steady your nerves under normal conditions, but these are not normal conditions. The heat from studio lights, the electric atmosphere, the unusual circumstances, all serve to increase the tension and may cause any alcohol in your system to have adverse effects on you. Keep a clear head, and be sure to visit the lavatory before the interview. The more comfortable you are, the more relaxed you will appear to be when the time comes.

Remember, at this stage you are a very important person. You will have cost the television company money already, and they now need you to do this interview, so if there is something that you are uncertain about or unhappy with don't be afraid to ask and have it put right. The last thing they want is for you to refuse to do the interview, so relax.

On the Air
Once the interview has begun there is no turning back. It is now that your technique is essential.

1. Sit comfortably, but do not slouch.

2. Avoid mannerisms. Speaking from a platform you may say 'yes' or 'no', nodding or shaking your head violently at the same time, but on television this can look somewhat eccentric. Try to keep your head fairly still. Keep your arms still too. If you wave them about it looks clumsy on the small screen and you are liable to knock microphones over if you are not careful.

Although your face should not be expressionless, attempt to keep eyebrow-waving and eye-fluttering to a minimum, as even the smallest facial gestures can appear exaggerated.

3. Don't move your head around too much. Some speakers seem to gaze at the studio ceiling, at the walls, the floor, above the camera, which becomes irritating. It often helps just to concentrate on the face of the person interviewing you, and look occasionally at the camera yourself as you speak so as to include the viewers at home.

Concentrate on the interviewer all the time he or she is speaking – the camera is sure to be on the interviewer anyway, and that will ensure that you will understand the questions.

The following rules for speaking on television apply to radio as well.

4. Show you know your facts by using positive short statements. Not 'Well ... er ... I think there might be about five hundred people involved. Maybe six hundred, I'm not too sure.'

Be able to say instead: 'Some five hundred people will be involved.'

5. Watch your voice. Speak in a normal conversational way and take care not to pick up the tone of the interviewer. First-time television performers, due to nerves, tend unconsciously to talk in the same tone as the interviewer, which sounds like mockery, or else they speak in a flat unvaried monotone.

6. Don't appear arrogant or a know-all. Be seen to be in command of the facts, but try not to seem pushy, presumptuous or patronizing.

7. Before you go into the studio think to yourself of the worst possible question that you would hate to be asked, and think of an answer for it. That way you will be prepared for the worst.

8. Be alert and confident in your speech. Weak and insignificant characters have vanished from the viewers' minds by the next commercial break, but one with authority will make him or herself noticed. Do not be afraid to challenge the interviewer if you feel that he is creating the wrong impression.

Interviewers will sometimes say: 'It has been said that ... ' Do not be afraid to ask who. The viewers appreciate it. On the other hand, if you agree with a statement then feel free to say, 'Yes, certainly ...'

If the interviewer does not ask the very question you would like, there is nothing to stop you getting *your* point over by saying:

'That is a valid question, but first may I point out ...'

'Yes, I'll answer that question in a second, but may I just say ...'

'I'm sorry, that question is totally irrelevant, the main issue is ...'

and bring the discussion back to your views, It is after all *your* interview.

9. With most other speeches, I have emphasized the importance of the finish. On television you are very unlikely to be able to stage-manage your own finale. It is almost certain that the interviewer will end the interview himself as and when time dictates – you could even be in mid-flow: 'I'm sorry, Mrs Brown, but I shall have to stop you there. Thank you very much. In Grimsby today the fishermen ... ' and a completely different topic will be on the screens before you realize it.

When you speak on television how you start is the important thing, for unlike an after-dinner speech, or a committee meeting, viewers and listeners at home can switch you off if they are not interested, so you must try to engage their interest straight away. That is why it is good to try to find out what your first question will be before you begin. The first twenty seconds are vital.

'No, I disagree entirely with that statement. What we have proposed is a measure from which the whole country will benefit ...'

One authoritative statement will capture the viewers' attention, or at least deter them from switching channels or going off to make a cup of tea.

10. Keep your sentences short and simple. A majority of your audience may know nothing about the issue in question, they may never have seen you before in their lives, and to hold their interest you must talk on such a level that everyone can understand.

The most effective way of learning is to watch television interviews yourself. Listen to what people say, how interviewees react, and which people hold your attention most and why. You will be able to see where others go wrong and how you can avoid their mistakes.

Radio

With radio, speech is your only form of communication – appearance, expressions and gestures are useless. Everything that you wish to communicate must be done with the voice alone. A good speaker will engage the interest of the listeners immediately, and can even attract listeners.

Some people will switch on while you are speaking, but whether they stay with you or turn over to Terry Wogan will depend on what you are saying and how you are saying it.

Listen to the way professional radio presenters speak – their pace, their nuances, style and vocabulary. The latter is important because you can manipulate it to make even the most complex of subjects sound simple. Fluency is essential too – here more than in any other medium of communication the 'um' and 'er' are strictly taboo.

Practise listening to people in queues, restaurants and the underground, *without looking at them*. See how much is conveyed about that person through their voice alone. How much is lost by not seeing gestures and expressions? How can this be compensated for in the tone of voice? Try to draw a mental picture of that person in your mind, and then turn to look at them ... you may have been completely wrong!

By listening to voices on the radio and in situations as above you will begin to notice the variety of voices and the difference that pitch, articulation, rhythm and speed of speech make, and that all important *pause*.

Radio Interviews

Speaking on radio does have advantages over television, especially for the first-time speaker, in that if your interview is to be recorded it can be done several times if you make a real hash of it, and you can have written notes in front of you to assist your memory.

As with television there are special points to note:

1. Keep your answers concise and easily understandable. It is even harder to concentrate on a radio voice than on a television picture if you use long sentences, so be brief.

2. Speak directly into the microphone, which will be on the table or hanging just in front of you.

3. Don't rustle your notes, sniff, clear your throat, cough, play with a pencil, or make any noises that will be picked up by the microphone.

4. Don't interrupt the interviewer when he speaks. This can be done to a certain extent on television, but not on radio as this blurs the two voices together and makes you both incomprehensible. By all means make a sign to the interviewer that you wish to speak, but say nothing until he has finished. Remember that on radio you cannot see who is speaking or which voice belongs to whom, so this must be made clear.

5. Do not take it for granted that you need not explain something in simple terms. There will be many listeners who know nothing about the subject of which you are speaking.

6. Always remain calm and friendly even if the interviewer rattles you. He is probably on the radio daily and is the listeners' friend, so do not upset him or be rude to him, or the switchboard will be jammed with complaints about you. However hostile he may be about your cause try to remain calm. He may deliberately attempt to rile you. Don't let him. If you turn out to be a good speaker, someone who handles questions well and who gets on with the interviewer, there is a chance that you will be asked back again.

7. If you are speaking on local radio do keep it local. Say 'Hospital workers in Berkshire are trying out this new scheme ...' Try also to use the word 'today' wherever possible. Radio is a topical medium: it is happening *now*, and rather than say 'Last week we ... ' say instead, 'Today we will ... ' which makes it

immediate.

8. Project yourself as a friendly person, even if you are talking about a serious subject. If it is local then mention local factories and businesses that people know. If you have the facilities to cope with the administration, don't be frightened of saying: 'If listeners would like to know more about this, they can always write to me and I will be delighted to deal with any questions ... ' This makes you less remote and within easy reach of the public.

Being a Phone-in Guest

Phone-in radio programmes are very popular, and if you are a member of parliament, in local government, a trade union leader, or a public figure of any kind you may be asked to do such a programme.

The difficulty here is that you can have no previous knowledge of what questions you will be asked by callers, so you must be well prepared.

The procedure is slightly different from that of a normal radio interview. As well as sitting in front of a microphone you will be given a set of earphones through which you will be able to hear the questions. Listen carefully and jot the question down for reference.

You will then say:

'Hello, Mrs Jones, what is your question?'

'Hello, I would like to know why your men should be paid money when they are on strike?'

'Why should they be paid money when on strike? Well, the reason is because ...'

You will see that the listener's question is repeated. This makes certain that everyone at home is sure of the question, and by repeating it to the listener she will have contradicted you if you have heard it wrongly, and it gives you a few seconds to think of an answer.

Always be polite to listeners even if they themselves become offensive. Flatter the caller by saying, 'I'm very glad you raised that point ... ' or 'What an excellent question ... '. Keep your answers short. Refute any arguments with concrete evidence and your own point of view. If the worst comes to the worst you can always say: 'I do hope that answers your question. Next caller please ... ' before they have an opportunity to contradict you.

Speaking on radio can be great fun, and it is an ideal method of reaching a mass audience in a manner that would otherwise be impossible.

Television and Radio Station Addresses
If you are planning to approach a television or radio station, it is always best to write to the producer of the specific programme in which you are interested.

BBC Television Centres

London	BBC Television Centre Wood Lane London WL2 7RJ
Birmingham	Broadcasting Centre Pebble Mill Road Birmingham B5 7QQ
Manchester	New Broadcasting House Oxford Road Manchester M60 1SJ
Bristol	Broadcasting House 21-33b Whiteladies Road Clifton Bristol BS8 2LR

BBC Regional Television Stations

East	St Catherine's Close All Saints' Green Norwich NR1 3ND
Midlands	Broadcasting Centre Pebble Mill Road Birmingham B5 7QQ

North	Broadcasting Centre Woodhouse Lane Leeds LS2 9PX
North East	Broadcasting House 54 New Bridge Street Newcastle-upon-Tyne NE1 8AA
North West	New Broadcasting House Oxford Road Manchester M60 1SJ
Northern Ireland	Broadcasting House 25-27 Ormeau Avenue Belfast BT2 8HQ
Scotland	Broadcasting House Queen Margaret Drive Glasgow G12 8DG
	Broadcasting House 5 Queen Street Edinburgh EH2 1JF
	Broadcasting House Beechgrove Terrace Aberdeen AB9 2TZ
South	South Western House Canute Road Southampton SO9 1PF
South West	Broadcasting House Seymour Road Mannamead, Plymouth PL3 5BD

West   Broadcasting House
                        21-33b Whiteladies Road
                        Clifton
                        Bristol BS8 2LR

Independent Television Companies

                        Anglia Television Ltd
                        Anglia House
                        Norwich NR1 3JG

                        Border Television Ltd
                        The Television Centre
                        Carlisle CA1 3NT

                        Central Television PLC
                        Broad Street
                        Birmingham B1 2JP

                        Channel Television
                        The Television Centre
                        St Helier
                        Jersey, C.I.

                        Grampian Television Ltd
                        Queens Cross
                        Aberdeen AB9 2XJ

                        Granada Television Ltd
                        TC Centre
                        Manchester M60 9EA

                        HTV Ltd
                        The Television Centre
                        Cardiff CF1 9XL

                        London Weekend Television Ltd
                        South Bank Television Centre
                        Kent House

Upper Ground
London SE1 9LT

Scottish Television Ltd
Cowcaddens
Glasgow G2 3PR

TV-AM
Breakfast Television Centre
Hawley Crescent
London NW1 8EF

Television South PLC
Northam
Southampton SO9 4YQ

Television South West Ltd
Derry's Cross
Plymouth PL1 2SP

Thames Television Ltd
Teddington Lock
Teddington
Middlesex TW11 9NT

Tyne Tees Television Ltd
Television Centre
City Road
Newcastle-upon-Tyne NE1 2AL

Ulster Television Ltd
Havelock House
Ormeau Road
Belfast BT7 1EB

Yorkshire Television Ltd
Television Centre
Leeds LS3 1JS

BBC Radio

London	British Broadcasting Corporation
	Broadcasting House
	London W1A 1AA

BBC Local Radio Stations

Birmingham	BBC Radio Birmingham
	Pebble Mill Road
	Birmingham B5 7SA
Blackburn	BBC Radio Blackburn
	King Street
	Blackburn
	Lancs BB2 2BA
Brighton	BBC Radio Brighton
	Marlborough Place
	Brighton
	Sussex BN1 1TU
Bristol	BBC Radio Bristol
	3 Tyndalls Park Road
	Bristol BS8 1PP
Cambridgeshire	BBC Radio Cambridgeshire
	Broadcasting House
	104 Hills Road
	Cambridge CB2 1LD
Carlisle	BBC Radio Carlisle
	Hilltop Heights
	London Road
	Carlisle CA1 2NA

Cleveland	BBC Radio Cleveland 91-93 Linthorpe Road Middlesborough Teesside Cleveland TS1 5DG
Derby	BBC Radio Derby 56 St Helen's Street Derby DE1 3HY
Humberside	BBC Radio Humberside 9 Chapel Street Hull HU1 3NU
Leeds	BBC Radio Leeds Broadcasting House Woodhouse Lane Leeds LC2 2PN
Leicester	BBC Radio Leicester Epic House Charles Street Leicester LE1 3SH
Lincolnshire	BBC Radio Lincolnshire Radion Buildings Lincoln LN1 3DF
London	BBC Radio London 35a Marylebone High Street London W1A 4LG
Manchester	BBC Radio Manchester P.O. Box 90 New Broadcasting House Oxford Road Manchester M60 1SJ

Medway	BBC Radio Medway 30 High Street Chatham Kent ME4 4EZ
Merseyside	BBC Radio Merseyside Commerce House 13-17 Sir Thomas Street Liverpool L1 5BS
Newcastle	BBC Radio Newcastle Crestina House Archbold Terrace Newcastle-upon-Tyne NE2 1DZ
Norfolk	BBC Radio Norfolk Norfolk Towers Surrey Street Norwich NR1 3PA
Northampton	BBC Radio Northampton Compton House Abingdon Street Northampton
Nottingham	BBC Radio Nottingham York House York Street Nottingham NG1 3JB
Oxford	BBC Radio Oxford 242-254 Banbury Road Oxford OX2 7DW
Sheffield	BBC Radio Sheffield Ashdell Grove 60 Westbourne Road Sheffield, S10 2QU

Solent	BBC Radio Solent
	South Western House
	Canute Road
	Southampton SO9 4PJ
Stoke-on-Trent	BBC Radio Stoke-on-Trent
	Conway House
	Cheapside Hanley
	Stoke-on-Trent
	Staffs ST1 1JJ

Independent Local Radio

Aberdeen	North Sound
	45 Kings Gate
	Aberdeen AB2 OB1
Ayr	West Sound
	Radio House
	54 Holmston Road
	Ayr KA7 3BD
Belfast	Downtown Radio
	P.O. Box 293
	Newtownards
	Co. Down
Birmingham	BRMB Radio
	Radio House
	P.O. Box 555
	Birmingham B6 4BX
Bournemouth	Two Counties Radio
	5 Southcote Road
	Bournemouth
	BH1 3SH

Bradford	Pennine Radio
	P.O. Box 235
	Pennine House
	Forster Square
	Bradford BD1 5NP
Bristol	Radio West
	P.O. Box 963
	Bristol BS99 7SN
Bury St Edmunds	Saxon Radio
	Electric House
	Lloyds Avenue
	Ipswich IP1 3HZ
Cardiff	Cardiff Broadcasting Company
	Radio House
	West Canal Wharf
	Cardiff
Coventry	Mercia Sound
	Hertford Place
	Coventry CV1 3TT
Dundee & Perth	Taysound Broadcasting
	P.O. Box 123
	Dundee DD1 9UF
Edinburgh	Radio Forth
	Forth House
	Forth Street
	Edinburgh EH1 3LF
Exeter & Torbay	Devon Air Radio
	35-37 St David's Hill
	Exeter EX4 4DA

Glasgow	Radio Clyde Ranken House Blythswood Court Anderson Cross Centre Glasgow G2 7LB
Gloucester & Cheltenham	Gloucestershire Broadcasting Company P.O. Box 388 Gloucester GL1 1TX
Hereford & Worcester	Radio Wyvern Garnous Hereford HR4 7JT
Inverness	Moray Firth Radio P.O. Box 271 Inverness
Ipswich	Radio Orwell Electric House Lloyds Avenue Ipswich IP1 3HZ
Leeds	Radio Aire P.O. Box 362 51 Burley Road Leeds LS3 1LR
Leicester	Centre Radio Granville House Granville Road Leicester LE1 7RW
Liverpool	Radio City P.O. Box 194 8-10 Stanley Street Liverpool L69 1LD

London	Capital Radio Euston Tower London NW1 3DR
	London Broadcasting Company Gough Square London EC4P 4LP
Londonderry	Northside Sound 1 St. Columb's Court Londonderry
Luton & Bedford	Chiltern Radio Chiltern Road Dunstable LU6 1HQ
Manchester	Piccadilly Radio 127-131 The Piazza Piccadilly Plaza Manchester M1 4AW
Nottingham	Radio Trent 29-31 Castle Gate Nottingham NG1 7AP
Peterborough	Hereward Radio P.O. Box 225 Peterborough Cambs PE1 1JX
Plymouth	Plymouth Sound Earl's Acre Alma Road Plymouth PL3 4HX
Portsmouth	Radio Victory P.O. Box 257 Portsmouth PO1 5RT

Preston & Blackpool	Red Rose Radio 68 Topping Street Blackpool FY1 3AQ
Reading	Radio 210 Thames Valley P.O. Box 210 Reading RG3 5RZ
Sheffield & Rotherham	Radio Hallam P.O. Box 194 Hartshead Sheffield S1 1GP
Southend & Chelmsford	Essex Radio Radio House Clifftown Road Southend-on-Sea SS1 1AW
Swansea	Swansea Sound Victoria Road Gowerton Swansea SA4 3AB
Swindon & West Wilts	Wiltshire Radio Ltd 41 New Road Chippenham Wiltshire SN15 1HI
Teesside	Radio Tees 74 Dovecot Street Stockton-on-Tees Cleveland TS18 1HB
Tyne & Wear	Metro Radio Newcastle-upon-Tyne NE99 1BB

Wolverhampton & the Black Country	Beacon Radio 303 P.O. Box 303 267 Tettenhall Road Wolverhampton WV6 0DQ
Wrexham & Deeside	Marcher Sound Gororau c/o Hillview 11 Warren Drive Prestatyn Clwyd CL19 7HT

In all cases a stamped addressed envelope is advisable and will at least ensure that you get some sort of reply.

APPENDICES

1: Forms of Address

When making all but the most informal impromptu speeches, it is customary to begin by addressing your hosts, the guests of honour and the audience. It is important to get it right.

Royalty
Her Majesty the Queen. Begin: 'Your Majesty, Mr Chairman ...'
If you should address the Queen directly during your speech, on the first occasion you say, 'Your Majesty' and on subsequent occasions you should say 'Ma'am' (*Note:* pronunciation should be 'Ma'am' to rhyme with 'lamb' and *not* with 'harm'.)

Queen Elizabeth the Queen Mother. As above.

His Royal Highness, Prince Philip, Duke of Edinburgh. 'May it please Your Royal Highness, Mr Chairman ... ' If addressing Prince Philip directly, on the first occasion you say 'Your Royal Highness', and from then onwards, 'Sir'.

His Royal Highness, Prince Charles, Prince of Wales. As above.

Her Royal Highness, Diana, Princess of Wales. 'May it please your Royal Highness, Mr Chairman ... ' Addressed directly as 'Your Royal Highness' the first time and subsequently 'Ma'am'.

All immediate members of the royal family as above.

Chairman
If no royalty are present (and it is unlikely that there will be at every speech you make) you always mention the chairman first. So you begin, for example, 'Mr Chairman, Mr Mayor ...' Very occasionally the chairman may happen to be a peer himself, in which case you say: 'My Lord and Chairman ...' And should he be the president of the organization, it should be 'Mr President, ladies and gentlemen ...'

The Peerage

Duke	'My Lord Duke' or 'Your Grace'
Marquess	'My Lord Marquess'
Earl Viscount Baron	'My Lord'
Duchess	'Your Grace'
Marchioness Countess Viscountess Baroness	'My Lady'

Knights
Addressed as 'Sir', and if addressed directly the surname is dropped so that he becomes 'Sir Kenneth' or 'Sir Robert'.

Prime Minister
'Mr (or Madam) Prime Minister' or 'Prime Minister'.

Clergy

Archbishop	'Your Grace'
Bishop	'My Lord'
Dean	'Dean'

Provost	'Mr Provost' or 'Provost'
Archdeacon	'Mr Archdeacon' or 'Archdeacon'
Prebendary	'Prebendary'
Vicar or rector	'Mr –' or 'Father –'
Chief rabbi	'Chief Rabbi'
Rabbi	'Rabbi –'

Diplomatic

Ambassador	'Your Excellency'
Minister	'Minister' or by name
Chargé d'affaires and acting high commissioners	'Chargé d'Affaires' (or 'Excellency' – but this is a courtesy title only) or by name

Civic

Lord mayor	'My Lord Mayor' or 'Your Worship'
Lady mayoress	'My Lady Mayoress'
Mayor of city or borough (even if the mayor is a woman, although 'Madam Mayor' is now acceptable)	'Mr Mayor'
Chairman	'Mr Chairman'

Academic

Chancellor of a university	'Mr Chancellor'
Vice-chancellor	'Mr Vice-Chancellor'

Lesser titles can be embraced in the opening sentence: 'Mr Chairman, my lords, ladies and gentlemen'.

Of course, many organizations have their own forms of address, which you should do your best to master if you are unfamiliar with them.

In general, detailed formality in subsequent references to lesser titles can be dispensed with nowadays, though it is best to check beforehand whether offence would be given if Lord High-up or Sir Algy Snooks were not shown sufficient deference throughout your speech.

2: Source Material

I know of hundreds, and there are probably thousands, of collections of quotations, anecdotes and jokes that could be of value to public speakers. The two dozen books listed here are simply ones that I have come across and found both useful and entertaining.

Auden, W.H. & Kronenberger, Louis, *The Faber Book of Aphorisms*, Faber and Faber

Bartlett, John, *Familiar Quotations*, Macmillan

Cagney, Peter, *The Book of Wit and Humour*, A. Thomas

Cohen, J.M. & M.J., *The Penguin Dictionary of Modern Quotations*, Penguin

Cohen, J.M. & M.J., *The Penguin Dictionary of Quotations*, Penguin

Copeland, Lewis & Faye, *10,000 Jokes, Toasts and Stories*, Doubleday

Copeland, Lewis & Lamin, Lawrence W., *The World's Great Speeches*, Dover Publications

Edwards, Kenneth, *I Wish I'd Said That*, Abelard

Edwards, Kenneth, *I Wish I'd Said That Too*, Abelard

Edwards, Kenneth, *More Things I Wish I'd Said*, Abelard

Fuller, Edmund, *2500 Anecdotes For All Occasions*, Avenel Books

Goldstein-Jackson, Kevin, *The Right Joke For The Right Occasion*, Elliot Right Way Books

Green, Jonathan, *A Dictionary of Contemporary Quotations*, Pan

Green, Jonathan, *Famous Last Words*, Pan

Lieberman, Gerald, F., *3500 Good Jokes For Speakers*, Doubleday

Newman, A.C.H., *Newman's Joke and Story Book*, Elliott Right Way Books

Oxford Dictionary of Quotations, Oxford University Press

Peter, Laurence J., *Quotations For Our Time*, Souvenir Press

Rossiter, Leonard, *The Lowest Form Of Wit*, J.M. Dent

Tripp, Rhoda, Thomas, *The International Thesaurus of Quotations*, Penguin

Williams, Kenneth, *Acid Drops*, J.M. Dent

Wintle, Justin, & Kenin, Richard, *The Dictionary of Biographical Quotation*, Routledge & Kegan Paul

Kent Wright, C., *Unaccustomed as I Am*, George Allen & Unwin

Yarwood, Mike, *Just Joking*, J.M. Dent

3: Agencies for Professional Speakers

If you want to engage the services of a professional speaker – or if you are interested in the possibility of becoming one – you will find that a wide range of advertising and public relations companies, conference organizers and theatrical agents handle professional speakers, but among the leading specialists in the field are:

After Dinner Speakers
1 St James's Street
London SW1

Associated Speakers
24a Park Road
Hayes
Middlesex

Foyles Lecture Agency
119 Charing Cross Road
London WC2

Prime Performers
The Studio
5 Kidderpore Avenue
London NW3

These are all national organizations. There are also a number of local agencies in different parts of the country and for the addresses of these consult the Yellow Pages directory in your area.